Patti,

This book has been helping me
Through troubled times.

I hope it will do the same for you.

Jseti

# OUR DAILY BREAD

Francisco Cândido Xavier

# OUR DAILY BREAD

## BY THE SPIRIT EMMANUEL

TRANSLATED BY JUSSARA KORNGOLD

INTERNATIONAL SPIRITIST COUNCIL

ISBN 85-98161-07-1

B.N.

Original Title:
*PÃO NOSSO*

Translated by JUSSARA KORNGOLD
1st Edition 2005 – published by the INTERNATIONAL SPIRITIST COUNCIL, Brasília,
BR. – 1st impression 1000

21-AM; 000.1-O; 4/2005

Cover design by: ALESSANDRO FIGUEREDO
Layout: CLAUDIO CARVALHO

Printed and bound by
the Editorial and Graphics Department of the Brazilian Spiritist Federation
*Rua Souza Valente, 17*
*20941-040 – Rio de Janeiro, RJ – Brasil*
*CNPJ nº 33.644.857/0002-84      I.E. nº 81.600.503*

CIP-BRASIL. CATALOGAÇÃO-NA-FONTE
SINDICATO NACIONAL DOS EDITORES DE LIVROS, RJ.
E46o

    Emmanuel (Spirit)
        Our Daily Bread / by the Spirit Emmanuel; [received by] Francisco
Cândido Xavier; translated by Jussara Korngold. – Brasília (Brasil):
International Spiritist Council, 2005
        376p.:

        Translation of: Pão Nosso
        ISBN 85-98161-07-1

        1. Jesus Christ – Spiritualistic Interpretations. 2. Bible and spiritua-
lism. 3. Spirit writings. I. Xavier, Francisco Cândido, 1910-2002. II. Conselho
Espírita Internacional. III. Title.

05-0977.                                    CDD 133.93
                                           CDU 133.7

31.03.05   05.04.05                                        009669

# INDEX

# IN CHRISTIAN SERVICE

*"For we must all appear before the judgment seat of Christ,
that each one may receive what is due to him for the
things done while in the body, whether good or bad."*
Paul (II Corinthians 5:10)

There are some who undoubtedly perceive Spiritism as a simple experimental phenomenon of little moral significance to mankind.

Thus, many apprentices of this Consoling Doctrine limit themselves to laboratory investigations or philosophical discussions.

Notwithstanding, it is imperative that we recognize there are as many categories of discarnates as there are of incarnates.

Spirits that are argumentative, frivolous, rebellious and unstable are everywhere. Beyond these, other enigmas and problems appear to the inhabitants of both planes.

For similar reasons, the supporters of effective progress of the world, far from physical life, advocate Spiritism with Jesus converting the interchange in a factor of spiritual purification.

We feel that we should not investigate other circles of life, if we are not interested in improving our personality in the one in which we live.

It is of little value to search for resources that do not dignify us.

So for us, who supposedly have our hearts open to the responsibilities of living, Spiritism does not express just a simple conviction of immortality: it is a climate of service and edification.

It is of no use simply to have the conviction of the survival of the soul after death, without prior preparation for spiritual life while we are on Earth. In that effort toward rehabilitation there is no wiser and more loving guide than Christ.

Only in the light of His sublime lessons it is possible to re-adjust our path, renovate our mind and purify our heart.

Not everything that is admirable is divine.

Not all that is grand is respectable.

Not all that is beautiful is saintly.

Not all that is agreeable is useful.

The problem is not only to have the knowledge, but it is for each to reform oneself towards righteousness.

So let us adapt ourselves to the Gospel in feeling and in life, being mindful of our indispensable inner illumination because according to the opportune and wise words of the Apostle, "For we must all appear before the judgment seat of Christ, that each one may receive what is due to him for the things done while in the body, whether good or bad."

**EMMANUEL**

*Received in the city of Pedro Leopoldo – Brazil, February 22, 1950*

# 1

# LET'S GET TO WORK

*"What then shall we say brothers? When you come
together, everyone has a hymn, or a word of instruction,
a revelation, a tongue or an interpretation. All of these
must be done for the strengthening of the church"*
Paul (I Corinthians 14:26)

The Church of Corinth was struggling with certain strenuous
difficulties when Paul wrote the observation transcribed
herein.

The contents of the letter noted diverse spiritual problems
experienced by the Peloponnesian companions; however, we can
isolate the verse and apply it to various situations experienced by
Christian groups formed in a spiritist environment, in the revival
of the Teachings of the Gospel.

We usually notice intense preoccupation on the part of the
workers for news regarding phenomena and revelation.

Some nucleuses simply halt their activities when they do not have experienced mediums.

Why?

No medium can resolve, permanently, the fundamental problems of the illumination of companions.

Our spiritual task would be absurd if it were solely circumscribed to the mechanical frequency of many people, to any Spiritist center, simply to observe the efforts of a few.

May the disciples be convinced that the tasks and the realization belong to all and that it is indispensable for each one to work within the area of edification to which they are assigned. No one can allege an absence of new information when voluminous concessions from the superior sphere await the firm decision of the apprentice of good will regarding the understanding of life and the need for improvement.

When you meet, remember the doctrine and the revelation, your ability to speak and to interpret, which you already possess, and set to work of goodness and enlightenment, in the indispensable improvement.

## 2

# PAUSE AND THINK

*"The miracles I do in my Father's name, speak for me"*
*Jesus (John, 10:25)*

The preoccupation of the ordinary individual relative to family traditions is commonplace, as well as in the earthly endeavors to which they usually lend themselves, exalting the conventional position that distinguishes their personality.

However, in true life, no one is known for similar processes. Each Spirit brings with him the vivid history of his own acts, and only by his own actions and achievements is he known for his merits or demerits.

With this disclosure we do not wish to affirm that the word is deprived of indisputable advantages; nonetheless, it is imperative to comprehend that the verb has tremendous potential, which we received by the Infinite Mercy as a divine resource. It is indispensable to realize what we are achieving with this gift from the Eternal Being.

In that respect, the affirmation of Jesus is dressed in imperishable beauty.

What would we think of a Savior who would institute such regulations for humanity without sharing its difficulties and impediments?

Jesus Christ initiated His Divine Mission among peasants and laborers. He lived among irritable Doctors of Law and rebellious sinners. He walked among the sick and the afflicted. He ate stale bread with the humble fishermen and fulfilled His saintly task amidst two thieves.

What more can you ask for? If you long for an easy life and distinguished positions in the world, remind yourself of the Master, pause, and think.

# 3

# THE PLOUGH

*"Jesus replied: No one who puts his hand to the plow and looks back is fit for service in the Kingdom of God."*
*(Luke, 9:62)*

Here we see Jesus utilizing one of the most beautiful symbols in the construction of the Divine Kingdom.

Without a doubt, had the Master so desired, He would have created other images. He could have alluded to the laws of the world, to social obligations, to the Texts of the Prophecy; however, He preferred to fix the teachings on simpler basis.

The plough is the universal tool. It is heavy, requires effort and cooperation among man and the machine. It provokes sweat and caution, and above all, it tills the soil for greater production. As it proceeds it prepares a cradle for the seedlings, and the soil relinquishes so that the rain, the sun and the fertilizers are conveniently utilized.

It is necessary, therefore, that the sincere disciple takes lessons from the Divine Cultivator by embracing the plough of responsibility through an edifying struggle, without letting go. In this manner, thus avoiding a grave detriment to "his own soil."

Let us meditate over the lost opportunities, from the merciful rains that have fallen upon us and have been lost without being advantageous to our spirits; of the loving sun that has been vivifying us for many millenniums, of the precious fertilizer that we have rejected by preferring lazy inactivity and indifference.

Let us examine all of these and reflect on the symbol used by Jesus.

A plough promises service, discipline, affliction and exhaustion; nevertheless, we should not forget that afterwards, the harvest and the crops will place bread on the table, as well as fill the cellars.

# 4

## PRIOR TO SERVICE

*"Just as the Son of Man did not come
to be served, but to serve."*
*Jesus (Matthew, 20:28)*

While in the company of the spirit of service, we shall always be well protected. The entire Creation reaffirms this truth with absolute clarity.

From the inferior kingdoms to the highest spheres all things serve in their own time.

The law of work, with its division and the specialization of tasks, is preponderant in the humblest elements of the various sectors of Nature.

This tree will cure illnesses, that other one will produce fruit. There are stones that contribute to the construction of homes; others serve as a foundation for road construction.

The Father designated the planetary home to the human being, whereby each object is found in its proper place, merely awaiting the dignified effort and proper word, in order to teach mankind the art of service. If provided with the gunpowder designated to spark the energy, and if this gun powder is utilized as an instrument of death to his fellowman, the earthly user is accountable, because the Supreme Being suggests that every action be in the practice of good, aiming the elevation and enrichment of all the values of the Universal Patrimony.

Let us not forget that Jesus worked while he was among us. Let us examine the nature of His sacrificing service and learn from the Master the happiness of sanctifying service.

You can start immediately.

A hoe or a casserole constitute an excellent way to begin. If you feel ill and unable to make a direct contribution, you can still commence by helping in the moral edification of your brothers.

# 5

# SALARIES

*"Be content with your pay"*
John the Baptist (Luke, 3:14)

John the Baptist's reply to the soldiers that beseeched his enlightenment, is a model of conciseness and good sense.

Many people get lost through inextricable labyrinths by virtue of deficient comprehension regarding problems of compensation in common life.

Some employees solicit salaries merited by cabinet ministers without realizing the great responsibility that frequently converts world administrators into victims of insomnia and anxiety, or martyrs of presentations and banquets.

There are learned men who give-up the peace in their homes in exchange for increasing their salaries.

Numerous persons persist anxiously and incredulously from youth to old age with afflictions and illnesses for not accepting the monthly salary that the human circumstances of life have assigned to them within the Unfathomable Designs.

It will not be due to excessive remuneration that the individual will be integrated into the divine spheres of life.

If one individual remains conscious of the duties he/she is to fulfill, then, the greater his/her income, the greater his worry will be.

For a long time, there has been a popular saying that "For a great ship a great storm will surge." The acceptance of his salary on the part of each laborer is proof of an evolved awareness of the justice of the Almighty.

Rather than trying to analyze the pay scale here on Earth, get accustomed to placing value on the concessions received from Heaven.

# 6

# Make use of the light

*"Walk while you have the light, before
darkness overtakes you."*
Jesus (John, 12:35)

A person who meditates will come across divine thoughts when analyzing the past and the future. He will find himself situated between two eternities, the days of yore and the days yet to come.

By examining the treasures of the present, he will discover precious opportunities.

In the future, he will be able to foresee a blessed light of immortality, while in the past he will perceive the shadows of ignorance, of malpractice errors, and badly lived experiences. The great majority of humans possess no other panorama with regard to either a close or remote past except that of ruin and disenchantment, which compels them to reevaluate the resources at hand.

In spite of being transitory, human existence is the flame that places each one in contact with the service needed for a just ascension. With this blessed opportunity it is possible to redeem, to achieve, to learn, to conquer, to unite, to reconcile and to enrich yourselves in the Master.

Reflect on this observation of Jesus and you will perceive His illuminated reasoning. "Walk while you have the light," He said.

Take advantage of the gift of time you have been given in edifying work.

Stay away from inferior conditions; acquire higher understanding.

Without showing signs of improvement and betterment during the march ahead, you will be dominated by darkness. This means you will annul your sacred opportunity and revert to less worthy impulses, thus regressing after the death of the body, to the very shadows from which you previously emerged, with the intent of conquering new peaks on the sublime mountain of life.

# 7

# THE SEED

*"When you sow, you do not plant the body that will be,*
*but just a seed, perhaps of wheat, or of something else."*
Paul (I Corinthians 15:37)

As we observe things, within the tasks assigned to Nature, the seed represents the sacred role of Priestess of the service of the Creator and of Life.

As glorious heir to Divine Power, it cooperates in the evolution of the world and silently transmits the sublime lesson full of infinite values to mankind.

It wisely exemplifies the need for starting points, the just requirements for work, the proper places and appropriate times.

Some restless and insatiable individuals have yet to understand the seed. They expect great accomplishments from one day to the next. They forcefully impose their tyrannical measures by the use of power and arms or, otherwise, they intend to betray the profound Laws of Nature. They accelerate processes of ambition, establish transitory control, glorify themselves over fictitious conquests, become aggrandized and fall without even succeeding in accomplishing any sanctified edification for themselves or for anyone else.

They have not learned the lesson from the minuscule seed that provides wheat for the daily bread and guarantees life in all the regions of planetary struggle.

To know how to commence constitutes an important service.

In the redeeming effort it is necessary not to lose sight of the small possibilities, such as a gesture, a conversation, an hour, a phrase, which can be the instrument of glorious seeds for immortal edification. Therefore, it is indispensable never to disregard them.

# 8

## ANXIETIES

*"Cast all your anxiety on Him because He cares for you."*
*(I Peter, 5:7)*

Anxieties trigger many crimes on Earth and are never constructive.

Invariably, the anxious man has all the odds against him.

In opposition to these anxious disquieting moments the lessons about the patience of Nature appear in every sector of human pathways.

If man had been born to be constantly anxious, it would be, as if to say that he had come to this Earth not in the category of a sanctifying laborer, but rather as a desperate unpardonable soul.

If human beings could reflect more sensibly, they would be able to recognize the actual context of service that the moments of each day can offer. They would try to be more vigilant, and give proper value to their own assets.

Undoubtedly the scenery changes constantly, obliging us to encounter unpleasant surprises, as a result of our inadequate attitudes while experiencing happiness or pain. However, an essential imposition of the Law obliges us to proceed daily in the direction of goodness.

Anxiety will try to coerce gentle hearts because the terrestrial pathways unfold many dark corners and almost unsolvable problems. Nevertheless, let us not forget the prescription that Peter has given us.

Place your concerns and disquieting fears in the hopes you have in the Celestial Father, because Divine Love desires the well being of all of us.

It is just to ardently desire the victory of Light, to persevere in search of peace, to discipline yourselves for your union with the superior planes, to insist in synchronizing with the more evolved spheres. However, bear in mind that anxiety always precedes a fall.

# 9

# PEOPLE OF FAITH

*"Therefore, everyone who hears these words of mine
and puts them into practice is like a wise man who
built his house on the rock."*
*Jesus (Matthew, 7:24)*

The great preachers of the Gospel were always seen as the greatest interpreters of Christianity in the gallery of venerable persons of faith. But this, however, only occurred when the workers of the truth, in fact, did not forget the need for vigilance, which is indispensable at the time of testimony.

It is interesting to note that among all of His disciples Jesus regards most highly the ones who not only listen to His teachings, but also, puts them into practice. From this it can be concluded that individuals of faith are not necessarily those who are prodigious in words and enthusiasm, but rather, who also show and project attentiveness and good will towards the teachings of Jesus, by examining their spiritual context in order to apply them in their daily tasks.

We are comforted to note that all those involved in the field of evangelical work will be guided toward the interior marvels of the faith. However, we must always point out the elevated wisdom of those of moderation who upon registering the teachings and advice of the Glad Tidings, carefully seek solutions for the problems of that day or that occasion, without ever permitting their achievements to take place outside of an indispensable Christian foundation.

In all tasks the use of the spoken word is sacred and essential. However, no student must ever forget the sublime value of silence, at the propitious moments, in the superior work of perfecting his inner self, so that reflections may be heard within his soul, thus guiding his destiny.

# 10

## FRATERNAL SENTIMENTS

*"Now about brotherly love we do not need to write to you:*
*yourselves have been taught by God to love each other."*
*Paul (I Thessalonians 4:9)*

A strong contradiction, which disorganizes human contribution towards the building of Christianity, is a sectarian tendency that annoys a great number of its followers.

If there were more reflection and more attentiveness to the teachings of Jesus, then, those unjustifiable battles would be defused forever.

Even today, due to the manifestations from the spiritual plane towards the renovation of the world, individuals and groups of people appear to seek formulas from the Beyond, which would enable them to enter the realms of pure fraternity.

What are the enlightened companions waiting for in order to effect true brotherhood?

Many people overlook the fact that legitimate solidarity is scarce in places where there is little spirit of service and where there is an excess of preoccupation with criticism. Many well-known organizations are drawn into disturbances and dissolution because of a lack of mutual help in the areas of comprehension, work and good will.

Is there a lack of assistance? No.

Every honest and generous project resounds in the higher spheres, luring cooperative self-sacrificing workers to its aid.

When there is an invasion of disharmony in an organization of good will, the individuals involved should blame themselves for not fulfilling their commitments or for their indifference in giving assistance and service. Let no one ask Heaven for recipes of fraternity, because the sacred and immutable formula is already known to us, through the words "Love each other."

# 11

## GOODNESS IS TIRELESS

*"And as for you brothers, never tire of doing what is right." Paul (II Thessalonians 3:13)*

It is common to encounter people who claim to be tired of doing good. Notwithstanding, let us be convinced that such allegations do not flow from a pure fountain.

It is only those who are seeking a specific advantage for their own interests with a desire for immediate gain that become tired almost to the point of desperation when they are unable to achieve their selfish goals.

It is indispensable to observe immense prudence when a particular circumstance causes us to reflect on the evil that is assaulting us, in spite of the good that we judge we have planted and nurtured.

The sincere apprentice does not ignore that Jesus has exerted His ministry of love, without exhaustion, ever since the beginning of planetary organization. With regards to individual personal cases, the Master must have felt the thorns of our ingratitude, on many occasions, when observing our backwardness in fulfilling tasks of personal illumination. In spite of verifying our voluntary and often criminal errors, He has never demonstrated impatience. Instead, He corrects us with His love, tolerates us with His edification, and extends His merciful arms over each renovating project.

If He has withstood us and waited for us for so many centuries, why can we not also withstand with enthusiasm whatever minor deceptions of a mere few days we must undergo?

The observation made by Paul to the Thessalonians is, therefore, very justified. If we become tired of doing good, such a disaster would certainly only show that, as yet, we have not been able to eliminate the evil within ourselves.

# 12

## HAVE YOU THOUGHT ABOUT THIS?

*"Because I know that I will soon put my tabernacle aside
as our Lord Jesus Christ has made clear to me."*
*(II Peter, 1:14)*

If on many occasions great Christian voices have referred to supposed crimes of the flesh, it is necessary then to mention the weaknesses of the "self," and the inferiority of our spirit. So, we must not falsely accuse the body, as if it were playing the part of insatiable executioner separated from the soul, who would then be seen as its prisoner and victim.

We noticed that Peter considered the physical body to be his tabernacle.

The human body is a conjunction of agglutinated cells or earthly fluids that are united under the planetary laws, offering the Spirit the saintly opportunity to learn, to value, to reform and to aggrandize life.

Man, frequently, as an idle and perverse laborer, attributes the evil qualities that are assaulting him to this useful instrument. The body is a concession of the Divine Mercy, so that the soul may receive preparation for the advent of a glorious future.

Rather than casting accusations at the body, let us reflect upon the millenniums spent in the formation of this sacred tabernacle in the field of evolution.

Have you come to realize that you are an immortal Spirit taking advantage during a specific time here on Earth, of valuable potentials conceded to you by God, in order to fulfill your work requirements?

Such forces have formed your body.

What are you doing with your feet, your hands, your eyes, and your brain? Do you know that these powers were confided to you in order that you honor the Lord through your own enlightenment? Meditate over these questions and then sanctify your body, thus finding within it a divine temple.

# 13

## INDISPENSABLE STAGES

*"Repent then, and turn to God, so that your sins may
be wiped out, that times of refreshing may come
from the Lord." (Acts, 3:19)*

The restless believers almost always consider that the task of redemption is processed in some conventional providence and that with little outward activity on their part, they would readily acquire the most elevated positions, close to the Divine Messengers.

The majority of the Roman Catholics fully believe in the exemption of trials through the performance of outward ceremonies; many Protestants believe that through mere enunciation of hymns, they are in tune with Heaven; and a great number of spiritists think they are intimately in tune with the superior revelations, simply because they have attended a few seances.

All the aforesaid constitute a valuable preparation; but that is not all.

There is an inner illuminating effort without which no man may penetrate the sanctuary of the Divine Truth.

The words of Peter to the popular masses contain the synthesis of the vast program in the essential transformation that each person will have to undergo in order to achieve the happiness of the union with Christ. There are indispensable stages for this realization, without which, no one will achieve once and for all, the eternal clarity of the culmination.

Prior to all this, it is necessary for the sinner to repent, to acknowledge the extent and the volume of his own failings, and to finally convert, in order to reach the relieving peaceful instant of the presence of the Lord within him. Once he arrives there, he will be rehabilitated in the construction of the Divine Kingdom within himself.

If you truly already understand the mission of the Gospel, you will identify the stage in which you find yourself, and you will be apprized of the service that you must complete in order to move on to the following one.

# 14

## PAGES

*"But the wisdom that comes from Heaven is first
of all pure: then peace-loving, considerate, submissive,
full of mercy and good fruit, impartial
and sincere." (James, 3:17)*

Every published page has a soul and the believer is required to investigate its nature. The sincere examination will immediately indicate to which sphere it pertains, whether in the destructive activity of the world, or in the center of construction toward the spiritual life.

Initially, the reader, a friend of the truth and righteousness, shall analyze the lines in order to judge the purity of its context, understanding that if its expressions were born of a superior fountain, he or she will encounter the unequivocal signs of peace, of moderation, of fraternal benevolence, of loving comprehension, and finally of the good fruits.

On the other hand, if the page reflects a poisonous human partiality, such a message cannot proceed from the noblest spheres of life. Even though, it originates from a supposedly discarnate of an elevated category, if the page does not bring forth harmony and fraternal construction, it is merely a reflection born of inferior conditions.

Scrutinize, therefore, the pages of your contact with the thoughts of others, on a daily basis, and be friendly with those that desire your elevation. You do not need to choose the ones that appear more brilliant, but rather, those that effect an improvement within you.

# 15

## THOUGHTS

> *"Finally, brothers, whatever is true, whatever is noble,*
> *whatever is right, whatever is pure, whatever*
> *is lovely, whatever is admirable; if anything*
> *is excellent or praiseworthy, think about*
> *such things." Paul (Philippians 4:8)*

All of the accomplishments of mankind constitute the result of thoughts on the part of human beings. Evil and righteousness, the ugly and the beautiful lived, prior to anything, in the mental thought of he who produced them, in the incessant movement of life.

The Gospel projects a generous route so that the mind of man may be renewed on the path to the superior spirituality, proclaiming the necessity of such a transformation towards higher spheres. It will not be by acquiring a higher intellectual level in Philosophy that the disciple will initiate his efforts toward achievements of this nature. To renovate thoughts is not as simple as it may appear at first glance. It requires a great deal of renunciation and profound control of one's inner self. Those qualities are not easy for one to achieve without hard work and heartfelt sacrifice. It is for this reason that many workers modify verbal expressions, judging that they have reformed their thoughts. However, at the moment of recapitulation, due to the repetition of the circumstances, the redeeming experiences, once again, encounter analogous disturbances because the obstacles and the shadows persist in the mind, as occult phantoms.

To think is to create. The reality of this creation may not come to the surface at once, in the field of transitory effects, but the object formulated by the mental forces live in the inner world, requiring special attention in the attempt at continuation or extinction.

The message from Paul to the Philippians is of a sublime content. The disciples that were able to comprehend the profound essence in an effort to seek whatever things are true, honest, just, pure, and lovely, cultivating them each day, shall have discovered the divine equation.

# 16

## WHO DO YOU OBEY?

*"And once made perfect, he became the source
of eternal salvation for all who obey him."*
Paul (Hebrews, 5:9)

Every human being is obedient to someone or to
something.

Nobody remains without an objective.

Even rebellion submits itself to the correcting forces of
life.

Man is obedient at all times. However, if he has not been
able to define his own submission as a constructive virtue, it is
generally due to being influenced by impulses of a lower nature,
resisting the opportunity for his inner elevation.

He usually transforms the obedience that could save him
into slavery that will condemn him. The Lord delineated the

graduation of the path; He established the Law of personal effort, in the acquisition of the supreme values in Life, and determined that man must accept this design in order to be truly free. However, man preferred to go along with his inferior condition and created his own imprisonment. The disciple must carefully examine the field in which he is to realize his own task.

Who do you obey? Do you perhaps first attend to your human vanities or to the opinions of others, prior to observing the recommendations of the Divine Master?

It is always advisable to reflect in this regard, because only when we follow the living teaching of Jesus in every sense, can we liberate the enslavement of the world in favor of eternal salvation.

# 17

## INTERCESSION

*"Brothers, pray for us."*
Paul (I Thessalonians, 5:25)

Many human beings smile ironically when we speak of the assistance received from intercessory prayers.

Mankind has become so habituated to automatic theatrics that he has difficulty in understanding the sincerity of profound spiritual manifestation. The intercessory prayer, meanwhile, continues to provide benefits of inalterable value. It would be unjustifiable to believe that this type of prayer would be a flattering praise intended for an earthly monarch in order to obtain certain favors.

A prayer soliciting an intercession is surely one of the most beautiful fraternal acts, and can trigger the emission of beneficial and illuminating forces. Such forces, when originating from a sincere spirit, go straight to the proposed objective as a blessing of comfort and energy. The results, do not occur as a gift, but rather, as a consequence of just laws. It is difficult for man to believe in the influence of invisible thought waves, but he is in the midst of sounds which his material ears do not register. He solely understands tangible assistance; however, in Nature one can observe venerable trees that protect and preserve grass and shrubs receiving life's blessing without ever touching their roots or their trunks.

Do not overlook the blessings of an intercession.

Jesus prayed for His disciples and followers in the culminating hours.

# 18

## TRIALS OF FIRE

*"And the fire will test the quality of each man's work."*
*Paul (I Corinthians, 3:13)*

In modern mechanized industry they make reference to the use of trials of fire in order to prove the resistance of its product, and upon mulling over the fact, let us be reminded that in the Gospel these trials were equally reported at least twenty centuries ago with regard to spiritual attainments.

In writing to the Corinthians, Paul perceives the human laborers constructing upon one single foundation, that of Jesus Christ; each individual, thereby, preparing his own realization in conformity with evolved resources.

Each student, however, shall complete the task of his choice, fully convinced that the era of strife will be acknowledged in each and every one's eyes, so that a just trial will ascertain his merits.

The evolvement of the world, in its material aspect can supply the idea of the importance of the achievements of such great nature. The Earth is replete of fortune, positions, values and intelligence that cannot withstand the trials of fire. As soon as the purifying movements come close, they precipitously descend the steps to misery, to ruin and to decadence. In the service of Jesus Christ, it is also justified that the student awaits the moment of verification of his own personal possibilities. Character, love, faith, patience, and hope, represent achievements for an eternal life, attained by the student with the saintly assistance of the Master. However, all disciples should rely on the required experiences that, at the opportune moment, shall ascertain their spiritual qualities.

# 19

## FALSE ALLEGATIONS

*"What do you want with me, Jesus, Son of the most high God? I beg you, don't torture me." (Luke, 8:28)*

The case of the perturbed Spirit who felt the proximity of Jesus, and received His presence with furious questions, presents numerous aspects worthy of study.

The circumstance of begging the Divine Master to stop tormenting him demands the attention of the sincere disciples.

Who could possibly perceive Jesus Christ as capable of inflicting harm to anyone? This case involves an ignorant and perverse entity who, in his inner delusions, had been suffering due to his own doing. But, the proximity of the Master, brought him sufficient clarity to analyze his torment, a conscience embroiled in a swamp of crime and shadowy defections. The light was punishing his interior darkness, revealing a tortured nakedness worthy of compassion and pity.

The picture is very significant of those who flee from religious truths of life, classifying its contexts in the distasteful elixir of anguish and suffering. Those spirits, indifferent and playful, usually affirm that the service of faith submerge a tearful path thus obscuring the heart.

Such affirmations, nonetheless, denounce them. On a higher or lower scale, they are companions of the unhappy brother who accused Jesus Christ of being a minister of torments.

# 20

# THE MARCH

*"In any case I must keep going today, and tomorrow, and the next day." Jesus (Luke, 13:33)*

It is always important to move ahead steadily in search of a definite spiritual edification. It is indispensable to march, overcoming obstacles and shadows, transforming all the pain and anguish into ascending steps.

Charting His goal, Jesus referred to the direction of the march to Jerusalem, where the final glorification through martyrdom awaited Him. But, we can apply these teachings to our personal incessant experiences, on the route to the Jerusalem of our own redeeming testimonials.

Notwithstanding, it is imperative to clarify the character of the journey in the acquisition of eternal treasures.

Many believe that to move forward is to take a stand of evidence in the world, acquiring transitory positions of greatness and bringing the wealthiest things into their personal circle.

However, it is not so.

In this regard, those so-called "routine men" perhaps have greater possibilities in their favor.

The dominant personality, in ephemeral situations, has the road filled with dangers, with complex responsibilities, and atrocious threats. The sensation of grandeur augments the feeling of the downfall.

It is imperative to walk constantly, but this journey compels the eternal Spirit toward the improvement of his inner conquests.

Very often, many persons who presume to be on the higher peaks of their trip toward the Divine Wisdom, find themselves practically paralyzed in the contemplation of "will-o-the-wisp fires." Let no one be fooled by these false rest stops.

It is important to work, to know, to illuminate ourselves and to attend to Jesus Christ daily. In order to fixate this lesson within us, we have been born on Earth, sharing its struggles, making use of the body, and on Earth we shall be reborn once again.

# 21

## DEEP WATER

*"When He had finished speaking, He said to Simon.*
*Put out into deep water, and let down the*
*nets for a catch." (Luke, 5:4)*

This verse leads us to meditate over the companions in the battle who feel as though they had been abandoned in the human experience.

A disquieting sensation of loneliness breaks their heart.

They cry from nostalgia, from pain, renewing their own bitterness.

They believe that destiny reserved the cup of infinite bitterness for them.

They recall with remorse the days of early infancy and youth, of the hopes destroyed in the conflicts of the world.

Intimately, they experience each minute the vague confusion of the reminiscences that increase their feeling of emptiness.

However, all mortals experience those bitter hours.

If someone has not as yet lived them at a particular place on the path, let him wait his turn, because generally, each Spirit leaves the flesh when the cold signs of winter multiply around him.

So, when your moment of difficulty arises, be convinced that it is to come to your soul the days of service in "deep waters," the time to search for true values, without the incentives of certain illusions from the earthly experience. If you feel that you are alone, that you are abandoned, remember that beyond the grave, there are companions who will assist you and wait for you lovingly.

The Father never leaves His children neglected; therefore, if you find yourself, at present, without domestic ties, without true friends in the transitory landscape of the Planet, it is because Jesus Christ has sent you into the deep waters of the experience in order to test your conquests in supreme lessons.

# 22

## FICKLENESS

*"Because he who doubts is like a wave of the sea blown and tossed by wind." (James, 1:6)*

Undeniably, there is a scientific and philosophical doubt in the world that, enmeshed within loyal hearts constitutes a precious stimulus toward the achievement of elevated convictions. However, Apostle James here refers to the fickleness in man, who, by seeking to receive divine benefits in the sphere of personal advantages, customarily pursues varying situations on Earth, in the area of intellectual investigation, without a firm goal of relying in the substantial values of life.

He, who tries to trespass several doors simultaneously, will be unable to cross any.

Frivolities jeopardize the people on every path, mainly, in work positions, in illness of the body and in affectionate relations.

In order for any one to be able to judge correctly regarding a particular experience, it is necessary to enumerate the years that he has spent living with its characteristics.

We must, above all, confide sincerely in the Wisdom and in the Mercy of the Almighty, understanding that it is indispensable to persevere with someone or some cause, which will assist and edificate us.

Those unstable people remain figuratively represented "like a wave of the sea blown and tossed by wind."

When you are of service or when you are waiting for the blessings from on High, do not allow yourself to be affected by an obsessive anxiety. The Father disposes of innumerable instruments to administer goodness, and He is always the same Paternal Father through all of them. The blessing will reach you, but it depends on you, in the manner that you proceed in the constructive struggle, persisting or not, confidently, without which the Divine Power will encounter natural obstacles to manifest itself in your path.

# 23

## It does not belong to all

*"And pray that we may be delivered from wicked*
*and evil men: for not everyone has faith."*
Paul (II Thessalonians, 3:2)

Directing his words to the Thessalonians, the Apostle of the gentiles begged them for their participation in evangelical tasks, so that the service of the Lord could be exempt from wicked and evil men, justifying the call with the declaration that faith does not belong to all.

Through Paul's words one can perceive his certainty that evil men would be nearing the nucleuses of Christian work, and that their malice could cause them harm, making it necessary to mobilize the resources of the spirit against such influences.

The great converted one, in a few words, engraved an infinitely valuable warning, because truthfully, even though the religious color will characterize the exterior dress of entire communities, but faith will belong only to those who strive without measuring the sacrifices needed to install it in the sanctuary of their own intimate world. The mark of Christianity will be exhibited by any person; nevertheless the Christian faith shall be revealed pure, unconditional and sublime in rare hearts. Many people desire its acquisition as if it were a simple bill of exchange while numerous apprentices of the Gospel utilize it precipitously, as if it were an errant butterfly. But they forget that if the necessities of the physical body demand daily personal effort, the essential necessities of the spirit shall never be resolved by idle expectation.

To admit the truth, to seek for it and to believe in it, are the requirements for all; however, to maintain a vivid faith constitutes the divine realization of those who worked, obstinately, and suffered to achieve it.

# 24

## PRODIGAL CHILDREN

> *"And when he came to his senses, he said: How many of my father's hired men have food to spare, and here I am starving to death!" (Luke, 15:17)*

Upon visualizing the figure of the prodigal son, all the people idealized him to be a man of wealth, dissipating material possibilities in feasts of the world.

But the vision should be enlarged comprising all the different mannerisms.

The prodigal children do not solely breathe where wealth is found in abundance. They are found in all the areas of human activities, slipping in diverse forms.

Some great scientists on Earth are reckless with their intelligence dispersing intellectually poisonous thoughts, unworthy of the privilege they were endowed. Marvelous artists, sometimes waste their imagination and sensibility uselessly through miserly ventures, finally falling into idle pursuit of relaxation and of crime.

All over we see these dissipaters of wealth, knowledge, time, health and opportunities...

It is them who upon contemplating those with simple humble hearts, marching toward God, possessed of true faith, go through the great anxiety of uselessness, and afar from the intimate peace, hopelessly exclaim:

"How many simple laborers possess the bread of tranquility, while the hunger for peace tortures my spirit!"

The world remains replete with prodigal children and hourly, thousands of voices repeat these same painful exclamations.

# 25

## ON THE PATH

*"Some people are like the seed along the path, where*
*the word is sown. As soon as they hear it Satan*
*comes and takes away the word that was*
*sown in them." Jesus (Mark, 4:15)*

Jesus is our permanent path toward Divine Love.

Along with Him follow, filled with hope, all the spirits of goodwill, sincere followers of the sanctifying path.

On that blessed and eternal path the seeds of the Celestial Light proceed for the ordinary man.

Constant observation on the part of everyone is imperative in order that the treasures do not slip by unnoticed.

The sanctifying seed will always arrive in the most varied circumstances.

Just as occurs to the generous wind that spontaneously spreads among the plants, the principles of life, an invisible kindness distributes in all hearts the opportunity of accessing the road of love.

Usually, the divine spark appears in ordinary daily activities, such as in a book, in an insignificant incident at work, or in the useful observation of a friend.

If harmful herbs occupy the soil in your heart, and if you have already received the celestial principle, cultivate it with devotion, sheltering it in the garden of your soul. The human verb may fail, but the word of the Lord is eternal. Accept it and comply with it, because if you flee away from the imperative of eternal life, at some point, the angel of anguish will visit your spirit, indicating new routes to you.

# 26

## IMMEDIATE TASKS

*"Be shepherds of God's flock that is under your care, serving as overseers not because you must, but because you are willing; as God wants you to be; not greedy for money, but eager to serve." (I Peter, 5:2)*

Naturally, in the realm of just possibilities, no one should deny help or assistance to the companions that solicit a reasonable request from afar; however, it is our obligation to pay attention to Peter's teaching, regarding our immediate tasks.

Some individuals deliberately give themselves to disquieting thoughts of dreadful events, projected by the sick mind of others, and that will probably never occur. They waste a lot of time suggesting formulas of action or in useless lament.

The field work of others and future occurrences, in order to be examined, always require a great deal of consideration and reflection.

Further on, it is indispensable to recognize that the difficult problem, at hand or at a distance, has the finality of enriching our own personal experience, thus enabling us to solve other and more intricate enigmas of the path.

It is for this reason that the message from Simon Peter is profound and opportune for all times, and for all situations.

Let us attend to the imperatives of the divine service which is localized in our personal landscape, not by constraint, but rather, with spontaneous goodwill, escaping more so, from our own personal interest, and firmly and attentively assisting in good causes, as much as possible.

It is sometimes reasonable for the individual to preoccupy himself with the world situation, with the regeneration of the collectivities, with the positions and responsibilities of others, but we must not overlook caring for "God's flock that is under our care."

# 27

## CRUSHING EVIL

*"The God of peace will soon crush Satan under your feet."*
Paul (Romans, 16:20)

All over the planet we can recognize the existence of an unstoppable battle without truce between the forces of good and evil.

The great conflict manifests in diverse forms, and in the whirlwind of its movements many sensitive souls invariably maintain themselves in an attitude of evocation to the protective geniuses, so that these might come to the arena to combat the enemies that torment them, in an attempt to overcome them forever.

Soliciting help or calling upon the law of cooperation represent laudable actions of the Spirit that recognizes its own weakness. However, insisting on the aid of others to substitute the efforts that correspond only to us to dispense, displays a false position, susceptible of accentuating our necessities.

Satan representing the power of evil in human life, shall be crushed by God; however, Paul of Tarsus quite clearly defines the place of the divine victory. The supreme triumph shall be verified under the feet of men.

When a human being, through his own dedication and illuminative labor, dedicates himself to the Father, without reserve, effecting His sacrosanct will, forgetting the old animalistic selfishness, and learning his great importance as an eternal Spirit, an he shall then achieve a sublime victory.

Our Paternal Father has already dedicated Himself to His terrestrial children, but few are the children that have dedicated themselves to Him. It is indispensable thus, not to forget that evil will not be eliminated superficially, but it will be so, under the individual feet of each and every one of us.

# 28

## TO WHAT END?

*"But not everything is beneficial."*
Paul (I Corinthians, 10:23)

There have always existed indefinable individuals who though they have not hurt any one, equally, have not benefited anyone.

Examined under the same prism, the activities on the path require a sincere interpretation so that they are not lost in uselessness.

It is perfectly correct for a human being to dedicate himself to literature or to honest business practices of the world, and no one will be able to contest the laudable character of these who conscientiously choose their personal line of useful service. Meanwhile, it will be justifiable to know the ultimate purpose of the writer or the purpose of the negotiator. Of what good will it be to the first, to produce great works replete with verbal refinement and theoretic outbursts, if his words are empty of constructive enlightening thought on behalf of the eternal plan of the soul? In what way will the merchant take advantage of his immense fortune achieved through hard work and calculation, if it remains stagnant in safes awaiting the folly of the descendents? In both cases, it cannot be said that each of those individuals were involved in an illicit activity; however, they wasted precious time forgetting the fact that minor accomplishments yield an edificating finality.

The laborer who is conscious of his required responsibilities does not deviate from the straight path.

There is much affliction and bitterness in the factories of terrestrial improvement because its laborers are primarily concerned with material gain, overlooking the purposes of such improvement. Meanwhile, projects and experiments are intensified, but the just and necessary edification is always missing.

# 29

# THE VINEYARD

*"He told them; you also go and work in my vineyard,
and I will pay you whatever is right.
So they went." (Matthew, 20:4)*

No one can conceive that an Earth so replete with beauty and possibilities could be drifting aimlessly, wandering in the immensity of the universe.

The Planet is not a floating ship without government.

Collective humanity is accustomed to falling into disarray, but the laws that preside over the Terrestrial Home are expressed in complete harmony. This verification helps us to understand that Earth is the vineyard of Jesus. Here we see Him working from the dawn of the centuries and here we witness the transformation of human beings, who from one experience to the other integrate into His divine love.

The beautiful parable of the workers enfolds profound concepts. In essence, it designates the place of the human services and refers to the voluminous obligations that the followers received from the Divine Master.

For the time being, men hold on to the illusion that the globe can be the stage of racial or political hegemonies; but, they will perceive in time the clamorous deceit, because, all the children of reason, embodied on the surface of Earth, have brought with them the task of contributing to the achievement of a more elevated pattern of life in the corner in which they transitorily act.

Wherever you are, remember that you are standing in the vineyard of Jesus Christ.

Are you besieged by difficulties and misfortune?

Work for the common good, even so, because the Father entrusted each cooperator with the just and convenient material.

# 30

## CONVENTIONS

*"Then he said to them, The Sabbath was made for man,
not man for the Sabbath." (Mark, 2:27)*

In this evangelical passage, Saturday symbolizes the organized conventions for the service of mankind. For these conventions, there are individuals that sacrifice all possibilities for spiritual elevation. Just as certain public service employees postpone indefinitely certain providences of interest to all, by virtue of the absence of a minor stamp, there are persons that because of trifles abandon great opportunities of uniting with the superior spheres.

No one ignores the usefulness of convention. If they were totally useless the Father would not permit their existence in the scheme of things. They are tables that assist in classifying the efforts of each one of us, schedules that regulate the allotted time to this or that matter. However, transforming their use in conflicting precepts or in an obstacle that cannot be transposed, constitute a grave danger to the common tranquility.

The majority of people respect them prior to their own obedience to God; nevertheless, the Almighty designated all the organizations in life to be for the purpose of aiding in the evolvement and perfection of His children.

The Planet itself was created because of mankind.

If the Creator went to such extreme lengths on behalf of His children, why do we resist in satisfying the divine designs while attaching ourselves to the inferior preoccupations of earthly activities?

Conventions can define, catalog, specify, and enumerate, but they should not tyrannize the existence. Remember they were put in your path to be of assistance to you. Respect them in a constructive justifiable way; but do not convert them into a cell.

# 31

# WITH CHARITY

*"Do everything in love."*
Paul (I Corinthians, 16:14)

At present there are many people who still do not truly understand the concept of charity other than the act of dressing humbly on Saturday and Sunday in order to distribute some bread to the less fortunate, or to await public disasters to manifest themselves, or to send moving appeals in the press.

We cannot doubt the good intention of certain groups worthy of praise; however, we must recognize that the sublime gift is of sublime extension.

Paul indicates that charity, expressing Christian love, should embrace all the manifestations in our life.

To extend a helping hand, and to distribute consolation is putting into practice the highest virtue. All this potential of the spirit, nonetheless, should adjust itself to the divine precepts, because charity exists in speaking and in listening, in impeding and in favoring, in forgetting and in remembering. Time will come when the mouth, the ear, and the feet shall be the allies of fraternal hands in the services of supreme righteousness.

Each person, just as each thing, requires the contribution of goodness in a particular way. Men that direct or are obedient beseech their beneficial presence, in order that they can be illuminated in the department of the House of the Lord, in which they find themselves. Without sublime love, there will always be darkness, generating complications.

From this moment on, partake of your tasks charitably. If you do not find immediate spiritual retribution in the area of understanding, be certain that the Father accompanies all of His children with devotion.

Are there rocks and thorns? Fixate your thoughts on Jesus and go forth.

# 32

# CORPSES

*"For wherever there is a carcass, there the vultures will gather." (Matthew, 24:28)*

In presenting the image of corpses and of the vultures, Jesus was making reference to the necessity of the penitent individuals that require the resources in order to be able to struggle for the elimination of the shadows in which they are immersed.

A swamp is not eradicated by showering it with flowers.

The putrid bodies in the field attract vultures that devour them.

That representation of such great significance symbolizes one of the strongest calls from our Lord invoking the followers of the Gospel toward the movement of sanctifying work.

In various circles of the revived Christianity many disenchanted followers have surged, complaining about the action from persecutors, obsessors, and executioners, visible and invisible. Some students affirm that they feel tied to these influences and confess being incapable of following the designs of Jesus.

However, much thought should be given prior to making assertions of this sort that, in reality, only signals accusations at their authors.

It is imperative to remember always that the impious birds will gather around abandoned carcasses. The vultures will seek out other regions when the field in which they were congregating is cleansed.

The individual who invariably affirms unhappiness creates the impression that he breathes inside of a tomb; however, when he makes an effort to renovate his own path, those dark birds of sadness will draw themselves farther away.

Fight against the cadavers of any shape that may wrap themselves in your inner world. Let the divine sun of spirituality penetrates within you. As long as you remain a coffin for deadly ideas, you shall be closely pursued by the vultures of destruction.

# 33

## LET US ALSO WORK

*"Men, why are you doing this? We too are only men,*
*human like you." (Acts, 14:15)*

The cries of Paul and Barnabe to this day resound amidst the
faithful students.

The Christian family quite often has desired to perpetuate
the illusion of the inhabitants of Lystra.

The missionaries of the Revelation do not possess
privileges regarding the services they have to accomplish. The
achievements that we could bring to mind as grace or special
prerogatives only express a most profound effort on their part
to learn and to put the teachings into practice, together with
Jesus.

Christ did not found a Doctrine involving gods and
devotees, individually separated. He created a vigorous system of

spiritual transformation for the supreme good, destined to all hearts thirsting for light, love and truth.

In the Gospel we perceive Magdalene dragging painful deceptions, Paul, pursuing ideals of salvation, Peter, denying the Divine Friend, Mark, battling in his own hesitations; but, even at that point, we contemplate the daughter of Magdala renewed and pursuing a redeeming path, the great persecutor converted into a messenger of the Glad Tidings, the fragile disciple being conducted to the spiritual glory, and the hesitant companion transformed into an evangelist for the entire human race.

Christianity is the blessed fountain for the restoration of the soul for God.

The error committed by many apprentices stems from the idolatry in which they become involved around the valiant exponents of living faith, who accept in the sacrifice the true formula for spiritual evolvement; they imagine them in fanciful thrones bowing at their feet, feeling confused, inept, and miserable, overlooking the fact that the Father concedes the required energy for a successful victory to all His children.

Logically, we should all pay respect to and love the great representatives of the Christian path; on the other hand, we cannot forget that Paul and Peter, as were many others, originated from the human weaknesses toward the celestial gifts, and, that the terrestrial Planet is a school of illumination, power, and triumph, any time that we seek to understand its great mission.

# 34

# A QUIET PLACE

*"He said to them: Come with me by yourselves to a quiet place and get some rest." (Mark, 6:31)*

The exhortation of Jesus to the companions is of singular importance to the disciples of the Gospel in all epochs.

It is indispensable to learn about the "quiet place" in which the Master awaits the apprentices for the constructive repose in His love.

In this precious symbol we find the intimate sanctuary of the heart, thirsty for the divine light.

At no time did the Lord make reference to the locations of solitude that would be conducive to meditation, where one could customarily encounter vivid reflections of human nature. He was referring to the silent chamber situated within our own selves.

Furthermore, we cannot forget that the Spirit thirsting for divine union upon emerging into a superior idealism encounters itself disturbed, in profound isolation in the world, in spite of being of daily service, and in conformance with the infallible plan from on High.

In the secret temple of the soul, Jesus Christ awaits us, in order to reinvigorate our exhaustive strength.

Men initiated the search for a "quiet place" choosing the shelter of monasteries or of rustic areas; however, the teaching of the Savior is not located in the external world.

Prepare yourself to serve in the Divine Kingdom, in the city or in the field, in any season, and do not seek senseless rest, convinced that, quite often immobility of the body is torture for the soul. Before anything else, seek to discover, within you, that distinct "quiet place" where you will find rest in the company of the Master.

# 35

# AN ACTIVE CHRIST

*"For God who was at work in the ministry of Peter as an*
*apostle to the Jews was also at work in my ministry as an*
*apostle of the Gentiles." Paul (Galatians, 2:8)*

Human vanity always pretentiously maintained the Christ within sectarian religious circles; however, Jesus continues His activities wherever the principle of righteousness flourishes.

Within all the avenues of terrestrial evolution, in sanctuaries and in academies, we see the presence of restless beginners, the false believers, and unfortunate fanatics who light the spark in the bonfire of opinions and maintain them. In spite of this, men of true faith come forth surging as sacred vehicles of the active Christ.

Simon Peter centralized all the Evangelical tasks of the emerging Gospel, readjusting the aspirations of the chosen people.

Paul of Tarsus was a powerful magnet in the renovation of the gentiles.

Through both, the Master expressed Himself with a sole objective: the perfecting of human beings for the Divine Kingdom.

It is now time to recognize the light of those eternal truths.

Jesus continues to work and His infinite mercy is revealed wherever love is erected toward the supreme ideal.

No one should feel victim to the unjust complaints accusing the sincere and devoted disciples of retaining divine privileges. Let each apprentice make every effort to establish, in his heart, the propitious atmosphere on behalf of the manifestations of the Father and His emissaries. Work, study, serve, and help others always, in search of the superior spheres, and you will feel the active Christ, at your side, engaged in everyday activities.

# 36

## TO THE END

*"But he who stands firm to the end, will be saved."*
Jesus (Matthew, 24:13)

Here we do not see Jesus referring to an end, which could symbolize termination, but rather as finality, an aim, and an objective.

The Gospel shall be preached to the people so that each one can understand and achieve the superior goals of life.

It is for this reason that only those incarnates that know how to persevere are able to break the bud of animalistic conditions.

When the Master applauded persistence, He was demonstrating the arduous tasks of those striving to achieve the excellence of the spiritual path.

It is essential to eliminate those false notions of gratuitous favors from the Divinity.

No one will be able to flee with impunity from the respective effort required of him for his task toward personal perfection.

The doors of Heaven remain wide open. They have never been closed. Nonetheless, in order for the individual to elevate to such heights, he requires wings of love and wisdom. For this purpose, the Supreme Being confers extensive copies of merciful material to all His children; but He also confers to each one the obligation of carving them. Such a task, however, requires tremendous effort. In order to finalize the goal, the contribution of days and lifetimes are recruited. Many persons become disenchanted preferring to remain stationary for centuries in the labyrinth of inferiority; however, the good workers know how to persevere until finally achieving the divine objectives of the terrestrial path, continuing the sublime trajectory toward perfection.

# 37

## IT WOULD BE USELESS

> *"He answered: I have told you already, and you
> did not listen: Why do you want to
> hear it again?" (John, 9:27)*

Very frequently, the main preoccupation of many religious
people is the idea of forcefully transforming their friends
into agreeing with their personal convictions. They usually
persist in long and annoying discussions, in an incessant play of
words, without achieving a healthy and edifying point.

The sincere heart renovated in faith does not proceed in
this manner.

It is indispensable to diffuse this false pride of superiority
that infests the sentiment in a great number of apprentices. As
soon as they reach new avenues of knowledge, in the gradual
revelation of the divine wisdom, the debaters with evil

inclinations are intent on hindering and interrupting their progress.

The reply of the blind man from birth to the astute and inquiring Jews plays an active role for the sincere disciples.

Logically, the follower of Jesus will not refuse an explanation regarding the Master, but, if he has already explained the subject matter, and tried to benefit the closest brother with the values that make him happy without achieving the other's understanding, why pursue it further? If a man heard the truth but did not understand it, he has all the evident signs of an individual displaying spiritual paralysis. It will be useless, therefore, for him to continue listening to continuous repetitions; because, no one can deceive time, and the wise man that challenges the ignorant person would be referred to as an insensitive fool.

Therefore, do not waste your precious hours on minute and repetitive elucidation with someone who is incapable of understanding them, before he is overtaken by the sun, the rain, the fire, and the water of experience.

You have a thousand resources with which to work, in favor of your friend, without inducing him to conform to your way of thinking and to your faith.

# 38

# YOUR PERSONAL ACCOUNT

*"And said: If you, even you, had only known
on this day what would bring you peace!"*
Jesus (Luke, 19:42)

The exclamation made by Jesus before Jerusalem, applies more to the heart of man, "the living temple of the Father," rather than to a material city, destined to ruin and to desegregation in the sectors of experience.

Let us imagine what the world would be if each human being knew his requirements for inner peace.

By virtue of a general lack of attention to this important feature in life, men have become involved in painful difficulties, accumulating deep debts.

Let us notice the assertion made by the Master: "had only known on this day."

These words invite us to think of the opportunity of service that we have at the present time, and to reflect on the centuries that we have lost. They compel us to meditate over the occasion for work that is always available for the diligent spirits.

The incarnate individual disposes of a glorious time that is momentarily his own, which was provided by the Almighty for his personal renovation.

It is important that each one of us recognizes what is necessary for our own tranquility. Each individual should observe a dignified attitude toward comprehending his personal obligations, and the phantoms of disturbances will be withheld from afar. Let each person care about his own particular affairs, and two thirds of the social problems of the world would be naturally resolved.

Pay attention to the minor needs of your immediate circle and answer to them in your own behalf.

You will not walk among the stars, until you have threshed out the humble path that awaits you.

# 39

## INVITATION TO RIGHTEOUSNESS

*"But when you are invited, go."*
*Jesus (Luke, 14:10)*

At all times, righteousness has constituted the divine fountain capable of providing immortal values.

The individual that reflects must have observed that the period of infancy is a set of calls to the sublime spring.

The sacred invitation is repeated year after year. It comes down by way of our loving human parents, our academic mentors, from healthy reading material, from the religious sentiments, and from our common friends.

Nevertheless, few intelligences do reach the youth with their attention fixated on an elevated calling. Almost all the people listen to the petitions from an inferior nature forgetting their precious obligations.

Notwithstanding, the calls still persist.

Here it might be a friendly book revealing truth, silently; there, it could be a generous companion who insists on the enlightened realities of life.

Rebellion in man, however, even after maturity, usually laughs unconsciously, continuously passing by in a compulsive march, in the direction of natural disenchantments, which will impose more balanced thoughts.

In the Gospel of Jesus, the invitation to righteousness is groomed in eternal truth. By accepting it, we will be able to proceed toward the encounter with our Father without hesitation.

If the Christian trumpet has already reached your ears, accept its truth without hesitation.

Do not wait for the thorns of necessity.

During a storm it becomes more difficult to visualize the port.

The majority of our brothers on Earth walk toward God under the ultimatum of much pain, so do not wait for the lashing from the shadows when you can calmly follow through the clear paths of love.

## 40

# IN PREPARATION

*"I will put my laws in their minds, and write them on their hearts. I will be their God, and they will be my people." Paul (Hebrews, 8:10)*

We will translate the Gospel
In all languages
In all cultures
Exalting its magnificence
Emphasizing its sublimity
Spreading its poetry
Commenting on its truth
Interpreting its lessons
Impressing it upon our reasoning
Perfecting our hearts
Reforming our intelligence
Renovating laws
Improving customs

And illuminating pathways.

But the time will come

When the Glad Tidings will need to be imprinted within ourselves

In the intimacy of our minds

In the innermost depths of the heart

Through words and actions,

Principles and ideals,

Aspirations and hopes,

Gestures and thoughts.

Because, truthfully,

If Heaven allows us to disseminate its Divine Message to the world,

One day we will be required to convert ourselves

Into the living examples of the Gospel on Earth.

# 41

## IN THE FUTURE

*"No longer will a man teach his neighbor, or a*
*man his brother, saying, 'Know the Lord,'*
*because they will all know me, from the*
*least of them to the greatest."*
Paul (Hebrews, 8:11)

When humankind eventually engraves upon his own
soul
The luminous sections of the Divine Law
Individuals will not reproach one other
A brother will not denounce a brother.
Prisons will close their doors,
Tribunals of justice will remain in silence.
Cannons will be converted into ploughs,
Armed soldiers will revert to tilling the soil.
Hatred will be expelled from the world
Bayonets will be put to rest

Machines will not hurl flames to ignite fires and death,
But rather, they will peacefully look after the progress of
the planet.
Justice shall be overtaken by love.
The offspring of faith will not only be just
But also good, and profoundly so.
Prayer will be of happiness and praise,
And the houses of worship will be consecrated to the
sublime work of supreme fraternity.
The preaching of the Law
Will live in the deeds and thoughts of all
Because the Lamb of God
Will have transformed the hearts of every individual
Into a temple of eternal light,
Wherein His Divine Kingdom
Will forever shine.

# 42

## FOREVER ALIVE

*"He is not the God of the dead, but of the living. You are badly mistaken." (Mark, 12:27)*

Considering established conventions with regards to our references to spiritual life, we usually utilize the word "death" in our common conversation. However, it is imperative to understand it not as a cessation, but rather, as a transformation of life.

Spiritually speaking we are only familiar with a terrible type of death, that of the conscience blackened in evil, tortured by remorse or paralyzed in the piercing precipice that borders the path of insensitivity and of crime.

The time has come for us to recognize that we are all alive in the Eternal Creation.

By virtue of withholding this knowledge from humankind, grave errors have been committed. For this reason, the Catholic Church created in its theology an artificial heaven and hell. Diverse Evangelical Protestant groups, more attached to the word, believe that the physical body, material clothing of the Spirit, would one day return from the grave, violating the principles of Nature. Also, numerous spiritists believe us to be laboratory phantoms or flickering forms, vague and ethereal, wandering indefinitely.

Whosoever goes to the grave continues working, and here, as well as there, disorder only exists for the rebellious. In the surface of the Earth or beyond its limits, we continue very much alive.

Do not forget, therefore, that the discarnates are neither magicians nor fortune-tellers. They are simply brothers who continue in the struggle to improve and perfect themselves. We encounter death only in the paths to evil, where the shadows impede the glorious vision of life.

Let us guard the lesson of the Gospel and never forget the fact that our Father is God of the living immortals.

# 43

## GOOD MANNERS

*"Take the lowest place."*
*Jesus (Luke, 14:10)*

In this passage the Master affords us an unforgettable lesson in good manners.

It is true that the context is highly symbolic with regard to the paternal banquet of Divine Mercy; nevertheless, it would be convenient to transfer this concept in order to apply it to the mechanisms of common day living.

The recommendation of our Savior applies to all situations when we are called to examine something new, brought on by our fellow man. For instance, someone who enters a home or participates in a reunion for the first time, with an air of superiority "a know it all attitude," and gives the impression of being from a better environment than that in which he is visiting, becomes intolerable to those present.

Even though it be a group misguided in its ulterior motives or finality, it would be unreasonable for an enlightened individual to become an austere and demanding counselor. For the task of rectifying or guiding souls, it is indispensable for the faithful worker of righteousness to initiate the effort, and reach out to these hearts through genuine fraternity. Only in this way will he be able to file away the imperfections effectively, thereby, eliminating a portion of the shadows daily, by way of constant service.

We know that Jesus was the great reformer of the world, correcting and spreading love, asserting that He had come to mankind to fulfill the Law.

Do not attack the places where you find yourself. When you stop somewhere with your siblings in God, do not overshadow them by exhibiting the extent of knowledge that you have mastered in the areas of love and wisdom. If you have decided to cooperate for the good of others, do not outshine, so that those around can truly understand you. By imposing rules or displaying powers you will accomplish nothing except to establish stronger disturbances.

# 44

## HEALING

*"Heal the sick who are there, and tell them,*
*The Kingdom of God is near you."*
Jesus (Luke, 10:9)

Truly, Jesus cured many of the sick and recommended them to the disciples in a very special way. However, the Celestial Physician did not forget to summon the Divine Kingdom those who were being restored in the human deficiencies.

It does not interest us solely to see the rehabilitation of the vehicle through which we express ourselves, but rather, above all, in the spiritual enhancement.

It is important for the individual to be free from illnesses, but it is indispensable that they value the health. However, it is extremely difficult indeed for us to understand the hidden lesson involved in the disturbance of the body, and difficult to assimilate the call to the sanctifying work to which we are directed for our physical equilibrium.

Would the Father allow the reconstitution of our cellular harmony solely, so that our contaminated will could strike it and injure it in detriment to ok spirit?

The patient will desire to readjust his vitality; nonetheless, it is up to him to be prudent and value the elements that have been delegated to him for this edificating earthly experience.

There are sick patients who lament being relegated to their bed and cry, not because they have renewed concepts regarding the sacred principles of life, but for not being able to prolong their reckless behavior.

It is always valuable to cure the sick when permission from on High is allowed; but because of this concession from the Almighty, it is reasonable for the interested individual to reconsider the questions that concern him, realizing that a new day was allowed to his spirit to proceed in a redeeming path.

# 45

# WHEN YOU PRAY

*"And when you stand praying, forgive."*
*Jesus (Mark, 11:25)*

A sincere attitude of the soul when praying is not derived from ordinary mechanical movements. During our common struggle, we invariably follow automatic material experiences that modify, almost imperceptibly, during our existence; however, when the soul turns itself toward the divine sanctuaries of the superior planes through prayer, our conscience becomes finely tuned to the eternal and creative sense of infinite life.

Let each apprentice examine the sensation that he experiences as he places himself in the appropriate position of prayer to the Heavens, being well aware that it is indispensable to maintain an inner peace, toward people and to circumstances on the path.

A mind at prayer moves continuously vibrating in the invisible sphere.

The incarnates, even though they are unknown to each other, concerning conventional activities, do communicate with one another via the delicate fibers of will manifested through the prayer. It is in such instances, that we should consecrate ourselves, exclusively to the most elevated zone within us, as we send messages, calls, intentions, projects and anxieties that seek a suitable objective.

Whoever utilizes this opportunity, consciously or unconsciously, to project currents of ill will, deserves our pity. For this reason, Jesus being aware of the lack of men and women free of culpability promoted this significant project of love to benefit each disciple of the Gospel: "And when you stand praying, forgive."

# 46

# YOU, HOWEVER

*"We who are strong ought to bear with the failings
of the weak and not to please ourselves."*
Paul (Romans, 15:1)

With what objective does the individual acquire the correct notion of faith in God? Does he do it to evade the struggle and subsist relying on Heaven?

Such an attitude would not be comprehensible.

The disciple achieves the light of understanding in order to put it into practice in his own journey. Jesus conceded him a piece of Heaven so that he could evolve and extend it while on Earth

To receive the sacred assistance from the Master only to remove it from the laboratory of redemption, is to manifest extreme ignorance.

To give oneself to Jesus Christ involves striving for the establishment of His Kingdom on Earth.

The earthly temples, due to the lack of understanding of the truth, remain replete with inert souls that deserted their service because of their desire to achieve blessings. This can be found in individuals who have not, as yet, achieved the necessary sense of reality; however, you, who are more versed in the knowledge of the Gospel, should not rest indifferently in face of the sacred duties of the shining light due to the infinite goodness of the Christ, in your inner world. It is imperative, therefore, for everyone to take hold of his work tools and to strive for the victory of righteousness within the circle of persons and activities that surround him.

Many sick spirits overtaken by false preoccupations and laziness in the world will plead ignorance. You, however, are not weaklings, nor are you lacking of the Lord's Mercy.

# 47

# THE DIFFICULTY OF PLEASING OTHERS

*"If I were still trying to please men, I would
not be a servant of Christ."*
Paul (Galatians, 1:10)

The sincere disciples of the Gospel would do well to preoccupy themselves with their own endeavors and conscientiously accomplish the tasks, which they were called upon to fulfill daily, learning to overlook the irrational opinions of the world.

The great multitude will not know how to display warmth and admiration except to those who supply their demands and whims. In the conflicts, which the apprentice will no doubt encounter on the path, the faithful disciple of Jesus will be a different type of worker who, instinctively, the multitude will not comprehend.

Great inexperience and lack of vigilance will be apparent to the messenger of the Glad Tidings who shows concern regarding how the world likes or dislikes him. When he finds himself in materially wealthy and prosperity, in which the Master confers him greater economic comfort, some malicious neighbors will inquire as to the cause of his successful triumphs; but, when he encounters poverty and difficulties, people will attribute these problematic experiences as a retreat in face of the sublime ideals embraced.

It is indispensable to strive on behalf of human beings, as one who is aware that the integral task belongs to Jesus Christ. The world will eventually recognize the great efforts of the sincere devotee; however, that will come at another time, when its evolvement permits.

On many occasions the popular opinion is equivalent to that of infantile gatherings who do not tolerate highly inspired educators on the subject of order and evolvement, work and achievement.

Let therefore, the sincere laborer of the Christ strive without concern for the erroneous judgments of the gathering. Jesus knows who he is, and that is all that matters.

# 48

# LET US UNDERSTAND

*"Sacrifices and offerings, burnt offerings and sin offerings
you did not desire, nor were you pleased
with them." Paul (Hebrews, 10:8)*

The ancient world did not understand the relationship with the Almighty except through magnificent offerings and severe holocausts.

Certain primitive people put forth sumptuously extravagant religious displays at the altars, involving human blood.

Such sad manifestations slowly dwindle through the ages; however, even today, some of these eccentrics and lamentable keen desires still exist in some areas.

Christianity brought about a complete renovation in the understanding of the Divine truths; still in some groups absurd promises sometimes surge which only favors the introduction of ignorance and vice.

The greatest notion of God that we could retain in the sanctuary of the spirit is the one that Jesus presented to us by revealing a loving and just Father who awaits our testimony of love and understanding.

On the very surface of Earth, any head of the family who is conscientious and strict, does not wish to witness his children in constant motion in useless offerings, with the thought in mind of altering the affectionate vigilance. If such initiatives are not agreeable to the human parents, who are capricious and fallible, how could we possibly attribute this fault to the All Merciful One, with the intent of achieving the celestial merits?

It is indispensable to strive to change this criminal deceit.

Genuine happiness is only possible in the Christian home throughout the world, when its integrants fulfill the obligations they are assigned, even at the price of heroic decisions. With our Heavenly Father the program is no different because the Supreme Being does not require sacrifices and tears, but rather, serenity in accepting His sublime Will, and putting it into practice.

# 49

## AN OLD ARGUMENT

*"At this point Festus interrupts Paul's defense: – You are*
*out of your mind, Paul! He shouted. Your great*
*learning is driving you insane."*
*(Acts, 26:24)*

It is common to hear the disciples of the Gospel referred to as crazy by the scientific circles of each century.

The argument is commonly heard from those who intend to flee the truth, complacent in their own errors.

There are many workers who waste valuable time lamenting over being referred to as mentally unbalanced by the multitudes. This is not cause for a sterile confrontation.

On many occasions the Master was assumed to be demented, and the Apostles were also thus defined.

In one of his final arguments we see the valiant friend of the gentiles, Paul, facing the Provincial Court of Caesarea proclaiming the immortal truths of Jesus Christ. The assembly is taken back in amazement. Those noble and sincere words frighten the listeners. It was precisely at that time that Festus acting as host of the guests, deliberately, tries to break down the vibration of astonishment that had come over the atmosphere. But before doing so, the astute Roman, realized that it was first important to justify his actions on a sound basis. How could he accuse the great converted of Damascus, if he Festus was aware of his correct character, his sincere humility, the sublime patience and the fierce spirit of sacrifice? He then, remembers the "great knowledge" and Paul was considered crazy by the divine science, to which he made reference.

Remember then the self-sacrificing warrior and do not be affected by false references from those that try to provoke you into abandoning the truth. Evil is incompatible with righteousness, and with little knowledge or with great knowledge from the moment that you align yourself with the disciples of Jesus, you will not be free of the inferior world with its sarcasm and persecution.

# 50

## PRESERVE YOURSELF

*"Go now and leave your life of sin."*
*Jesus (John, 8:11)*

The valuable seed that you do not care for could get misplaced.

The young tree that you fail to shelter is open to destruction.

The fountain that you do not care for could dry up.

The water that you fail to distribute becomes muddy.

The fruit that is not utilized becomes spoiled.

The good earth that you fail to cultivate becomes asphyxiated by useless weeds.

The hoe that you fail to utilize becomes rusty.

The flowers that you fail to cultivate will not re-bloom.

The friend that you fail to preserve avoids your path.

The medication whose proper dosage you do not imbibe as indicated will not benefit you physically.

Thus, as well, is the Divine Grace.

If you do not guard the blessings from Heaven respecting them in your own self; if you do not utilize the great knowledge that you receive to benefit your own happiness, if you do not appreciate the contribution that comes down to you from on High, then the dedication of the spiritual messengers is of no value to you. In vain, will they improvise miracles of love and patience in solving your problems, because without the adhesion of your will in the regeneration process, all their protective measures shall be useless.

"Go now and leave your life of sin."

The lesson from Jesus is expressive and sufficient.

The Divine Doctor provides the cure, but if we do not preserve it within us, no one will be able to foresee the extension and consequences of the new imbalance that will pursue us for lack of vigilance.

# 51

## SAVE YOURSELF

*"Preaching the good news of the Kingdom and
healing every disease and sickness."*
*(Matthew, 9:35)*

Seek a cure for your cataracts and your conjunctivitis; however, correct the spiritual vision of your eyes.

Protect yourself against deafness; meanwhile, correct your way of registering the voices and various requests directed to you.

Take medication for your arrhythmia and poor breathing; but also, do not yield your heart to move you impulsively.

Counteract the neurasthenia and the exhaustion; however, continually readjust your emotions and tendencies.

Pursue the gastric disorder, but educate your appetite at the dinner table.

Improve your blood condition; however, do not overcharge it with the residues of inferior pleasures.

Combat hepatitis; however, free your liver from the excesses that please you.

Remove the dangers of uremia; but do not suffocate your kidneys with the poisons in shiny glasses.

Dislodge the rheumatism from your limbs; but also pay attention what you do with your feet, arms and hands.

Cure the cerebral diseases that threaten you; however, learn to guard the mind in superior idealism and in noble acts.

Consecrate yourself to your own personal cure, but do not forget the recommendations of the Divine Kingdom directed to your physical organs. They are alive and can be educated. Without purifying the thoughts and without having your will commanding the ship of your organism toward righteousness, the use of all human remedies will be in vain.

# 52

## SUBTLE DANGERS

*"Do not be idolaters."*
*Paul (I Corinthians, 10:7)*

The recommendations given by Paul to the Corinthians should be remembered and applied at any time in the services of the religious ascension of the world.

It is indispensable to avoid idolatry in all circumstances. Its manifestations always presented serious dangers to the spiritual life.

The ancient beliefs are still replete with exterior cults and dead idols.

The Consoler who was sent to the world in the venerable spiritist mission, will watch out for this poisonous process which paralyzes the soul.

Here and there signs of worship surge that are important

to combat. No further use of idols in the human circles, or physical instruments supposedly sanctified for use in conventional ceremonies, but rather, friendly entities and incarnate mediums that unconscious individuals inadvertently introduce into the frail altar of the fanciful honors. It is necessary to recognize that there lies a subtle danger through which innumerable workers have slid into the cliffs of uselessness.

Inopportune praise customarily perverts the dedicated but inexperienced mediums, in addition to creating an environment of misunderstanding, which impedes the immediate interjection of the true friends of righteousness from the spiritual plane.

No one should overlook the relatively imperfect spiritual condition that, as yet, is held by the discarnates that communicate, and of the immediate necessities of life needed by the human mediums.

Let us struggle to combat the false idols that menace Christian Spiritism. Let each disciple utilize the ample resources of the law of cooperation, using his own personal efforts with sincere devotion to the task, and let all of us remember that in the apostleship of the Divine Master, love and fidelity to Almighty God will constitute the central theme.

# 53

# IN CHAINS

*"For which I am an ambassador in chains, so that
I may talk about Him fearlessly, as I should."*
Paul (Ephesians, 6:20)

In this chapter we observe the apostle of the gentiles
in an affirmation that, at first glance, appears to be
contradictory.

Paul alleges his condition to be of an emissary in chains
and simultaneously declares that this occurs, so that he can serve
the Gospel as freely as needed.

The great worker was addressing the companions at
Ephesus, referring to his distressing situation as prisoner of the
Roman authorities; meanwhile, because of this and the difficult
testimony, his spirit was more at liberty for the service that he
had to perform.

This panorama is significant for those who are waiting for economic financial independence or greater liberty in the world in order to exemplify the Evangelical Teachings.

There are many people who feel that they should wait for material abundance and earthly facilities in order to attend to the Christian ideals; but, this does not make sense. The service displayed by Jesus is designated for all places.

Paul, while in chains, seems to feel more at liberty to preach the Truth. Naturally, not all disciples will be crossing those peaks of testimony. But all, without distinction, bring along with them the saintly chains of the daily obligations in the home, at work, in the hourly routine, in society and in the family.

No one, therefore, should be intent on breaking the chains in which he finds himself, in the erroneous supposition that he will be a candidate for a better position in the work place of the Christ.

Only our duties correctly fulfilled will confer us access to a legitimate freedom.

# 54

# THE REASON FOR THE SUMMONS

*"So when I was sent for, I came without raising any*
*objection. May I ask why you sent for me?"*
Peter (Acts, 10:29)

The question that Peter asked the Centurion Cornelius is of great significance in apostolic accomplishments.

The Roman dignitary was traditionally known to be upright and charitable. He solicited the presence of the disciple of Jesus to attend to matters of a higher order, after receiving a generous counsel from an emissary from Heaven. In spite of that, upon arriving at the domestic circle, the levelheaded former fisherman from Capernaum asked: "May I ask why you sent for me?"

Simon desired to know the reason for this request as a vigilant worker would need to know exactly where he stands and with what finality he had been convoked to a foreign soil.

This expressive picture suggests many new ideas to the new students of the Gospel.

Many people desiring to hear this or that enlightened Spirit, which they have heard about, often invoke his presence in their doctrinaire meetings.

Such a request is innoportune and senseless.

How could we possibly request the company of someone who we do not merit?

We cannot attribute this impulse as frivolous, but we must try to evaluate the importance of the finality at play.

Let us imagine that you have summoned Simon Peter to a particular prayer meeting, and let us suppose that the venerable Apostle acquiesced. Naturally, you would be obliged to explain to this great celestial emissary the motive for your request. Reflecting sensibly, over our mental attitude, let us evaluate if we possess sufficient spiritual evolvement to see, to listen and to understand his glorious spirit. Which one of us could truly respond in the affirmative? Would we have the audacity to invoke the sublime disciple, merely to hear him speak?

# 55

## INVISIBLE THINGS

*"For since the creation of the world, God's invisible qualities, His eternal power and divine nature have been clearly seen, being understood from what has been made." Paul (Romans 1:20)*

The spectacle of the Creation of the Universe is the most outstanding of all the manifestations against negative materialism, son of ignorance or foolishness. The created objects more justly address the invisible nature.

Where could you find activity that unfolds without reason?

Every intelligent form was born of an intelligent source.

Mankind only knows the causes of his transitory achievements, ignoring all of the complex motives of each angle in the road. The exterior landscape that affects the senses is a minuscule part of the divine creations that sustains his habitat, conditioned to his possibilities of benefiting. The human eyes will not perceive farther then the limits of their capacity of resistance. The human being will live among the beings that he requires in his task of evolvement. He will have the adequate environment required for his needs of improvement and progress; but, let no one presume that the vital experience of the sphere in which he breathes is what his mortal fingers are capable of touching.

The visible objects in the area of illusionary forms are brief and transitory, resulting from the invisible forces of the eternal plane.

Fulfill the obligations that correspond to you and you will receive the proper rights that await you. Fulfill your daily obligations correctly, and you will not be required to repeat the same experience tomorrow.

# 56

## SUCCESSES AND FAILURES

*"I know what it is to be in need, and*
*I know what it is to have plenty."*
*Paul (Philippians, 4:12)*

In each social community there are numerous people that are overly preoccupied with their individual success, anxiously awaiting the opportunity for recognition. They are precisely the ones who do not maintain these distinguished positions for long, when invited to the most prestigious posts in the world, disastrously ruining the opportunity of elevation that life has conferred to them.

Those who have learned to live in poverty are usually the ones who know how to manage their material resources more effectively.

For this reason, accumulated treasures in the hands of he who did not work for it, often is the cause of crimes, separatism and confusion.

Honest hard working parents shall create in the minds of their children a mentality of personal effort and affective cooperation; while, the selfish and uncaring parents will foster uselessness and laziness in their descendants.

The lesson given by Paul of Tarsus in the church of the Philippians refers to the precious and indispensable lesson on the path with regards to equilibrium, demonstrating the need of the disciple regarding the value of poverty and of good fortune, of scarcity and of abundance.

The success and failure are two distinct cups filled with diverse elements that serve the same sublime finality. Human ignorance, however, finds in the first, the liquor of intoxication, and in the second, it identifies the bile for desperation. This is precisely the point where the profound error lies, because the wise person will extract from happiness and pain, from abundance or from scarcity, the divine contents.

# 57

# IN THE PRESENCE OF JESUS

*"Whatever you do, work at it with all your heart,*
*as working for the Lord, not for men."*
Paul (Colossians, 3:25)

The understanding of service to Jesus, among human beings will in the future reach greater depths for the glorification of the One who watches over us closely, and who has done so since the very first day, illuminating our path with the Divine Light.

If each educated person could ask himself regarding the essential reason for his activities here on Earth, he would always find in his inner sanctuary vast horizons of deductions of infinite value.

For whom has he worked in this century?

To whom has he offered the fruits of his everyday work?

We do not wish to detract from the respectable position of the countries, of the organizations, of the family, or of the personality; however, we cannot fail to observe their expression of relativity in time. In the course of the years, frontiers are modified, laws evolve, the domestic group is renewed and mankind progresses toward more elevated destinies.

Everything that represents effort on the part of man was accomplished through his own initiative in the field of permanent work for Jesus Christ. Whatever we have realized through the centuries constitutes a benefit or an offence to ourselves in the labors that belong to the Lord, and not to us individually. Legislators and governed people depart in time with their own individual baggage, and Jesus remains, in order to evaluate the advantage or disadvantage of the collaboration of each one of them in the Divine Service of evolvement and enlightenment.

Administration and obedience, the responsibility of tracing and following, are only subdivisions of the concession conferred by the Lord to the followers.

Dignified work is a saintly opportunity. Within the circle of service, the attitude of each human being will either honor or dishonor his eternal personality, in the presence of Jesus Christ.

# 58

## To Contribute

*"Each man should give what he has decided in his heart*
*to give, not reluctantly or under compulsion,*
*for God loves a cheerful giver."*
Paul (II Corinthians, 9:7)

When the affirmation given by Paul was divulged, informing that God loves a cheerful giver, many people solely remembered the material charity.

Praise, however, was not only circumscribed to generous hands that distribute small donations of goodness to the needy and to those in pain.

Naturally, all these demonstrations of love are recognized as divine, but we should note that the verb "to contribute," referred to in the current lesson, appears in all its grandeur.

Cooperation in righteousness is a palpitating matter everyday and everywhere. Any individual is capable of supplying it. It is not only the beggar who waits for it, but also, the cradle where all experience is renewed, the family in which we purify our virtuous accomplishments, our neighbor, our brother in humanity, and the workplace which signals our own individual achievements in our daily efforts.

At the moment of nocturnal rest, each heart can question itself regarding the quality of the collaboration in service, in the conversations, in the affectionate relationships and in this or that preoccupation of everyday life.

Let us be cautious of sadness and sterilizing shadows. ILL will, complaints, dissatisfaction, and frivolities, are not integrated in the kind of labor that the Lord expects from our activities in the world. Let us mobilize our resources optimistically, not forgetting that the Father loves the child that contributes with happiness.

# 59

## LET US PROCEED UNTIL WE ARE THERE

*"If you remain in me and my words remain in you, ask*
*whatever you wish, and it will be given you."*
Jesus (John, 15:7)

In the Lord's Prayer, Jesus explains to His followers, the necessity for the complete observance of the Father's designs.

The Master knew, that human will is still quite fragile and that numerous battles encircle the human being until he learns to establish a union with the Divine.

In spite of this, the lesson of the prayer was always interpreted, by the vast majority of believers, to be an easy recourse for obtaining celestial protection.

There are many who request special concessions and mechanically recite verbal formulas. Logically, they cannot receive immediate satisfaction to their personal whims because in the state of weakness and of ignorance the spirit requires, prior to anything else, to learn to submit to the Divine Designs concerning himself.

In any event, we will achieve the moment when our prayers are integrally fulfilled. We will accomplish this when we are, actually, spiritually in tune with the Christ. At that point, whenever we so desire, it shall be done; because, we will have penetrated the just reason for each thing and the finality of each circumstance. We will be capable of wishing for and requesting in tune with Jesus, and life will present itself in its genuine infinite, eternal, renovating and beautiful characteristics.

Whether incarnate or as discarnates, we are still walking toward the Master, intent on being able to experience the glorious union with His love. Until we get there, let us work and be vigilant, in order to understand the Divine Will.

# 60

## THE LOGIC OF PROVIDENCE

*"Remember those earlier days after you had received the
light, when you stood ground in a contest in the face
of suffering." Paul (Hebrews, 10:32)*

Those who cultivate sincere faith throughout the world, as a rule, are said to undergo great suffering.

In fact, there are those who affirm that they distance themselves deliberately from religious circles, fearing the contamination from spiritual ailments.

The godless, the ignorant and the futile exhibit themselves spectacularly, in the ordinary life, through bizarre shades of external fantasies. However when they get close to the celestial truth, prior to having access to the permanent happiness of a higher spirituality, they travel through great tunnels of sadness, downheartedness and taciturnity. This phenomenon, however, is natural, because there will always be reflection after insanity and remorse after excesses.

The problem, nonetheless, covers a greater circle of clarifications.

The mercy that is manifested in God's justice transcends human comprehension.

The Father confers to each ignorant or lost child the right to undergo the fiercest experiences only after they have been illuminated. Only after they have actually learned to perceive with their eternal spirit, will life offer them different values. The indispensable strength to triumph in the great battle over their afflictions will be born in their hearts from that moment forward.

The frivolous and opportunists, in spite of their appearance, are usually frail souls whose dry stems shall shatter at the sight of the first storm. The noble spirits that are able to withstand the storms of earthly trek are well aware of this. Only spiritual enlightenment will guarantee the success through the trials.

No one would yield the responsibility of a ship full of preoccupation and dangers to simple children.

## 61

# MANKIND WITH JESUS

*"Rejoice in the Lord always. I will say it again: Rejoice."*
*Paul (Philippians 4:4)*

With Jesus mankind rises
From the darkness into the light...
From inertia to service...

From ignorance to wisdom...

From instinct to reason...

From the use of force to righteousness...

From selfishness to fraternity ...

From tyranny to compassion...

From violence to understanding...

From hatred to love...

From deceptive possession to the search for imperishable
wealth...

From the bloody conquest to edificating renunciation...

From extortion to justice...

From insensibility to compassion...
From the shallow word to the creative verb...
From monstrosity to beauty...
From vice to virtue...
From disharmony to harmony...
From affliction to contentment...
From the swamp to the mount...
From filth to glory...

My fellow man, my brother, let us rejoice in the redeeming battle!

What an angelic pinnacle we shall be able to reach if we truly consecrate ourselves to the Divine Friend who descended among us and humiliated Himself for us?

62

# JESUS ON BEHALF OF MANKIND

*"And being found in appearance as a man, he humbled himself and became obedient to death – even death on a cross!" Paul (Philippians 2:8)*

The Master descended in order to serve,
From splendor into darkness...
From eternal dawn to total night...
From the stars to the manger...
From the infinite to limitation...
From glory to carpentry...
From grandeur to abnegation...
From the divinity of the angels to the misery of mankind...
From the company of sublime geniuses to living with the sinners...
From governor of the world to a servant for all...
From a magnanimous creditor to a slave...

From benefactor to persecuted...

From savior to helpless abandoned...

From a messenger of love to victim of hatred...

From redeemer of the ages to prisoner of the shadows...

From celestial pastor to an oppressed lamb...

From a powerful throne to the cross of martyrdom...

From a sanctifying verb to anguished silence...

From attorney of his flock to defenseless accused...

From the embrace of friends to the company of thieves...

From donor of eternal life to condemned in the valley of death...

He humbled and lessened Himself so that man could rise and forever shine!

Oh Master! What did you not do for us in order that we might learn the path to the Glorious Resurrection in the Kingdom?

# 63

## THE LORD ALWAYS PROVIDES

*"If you then, though you are evil, know how to give good*
*gifts to your children, how much more will your*
*Father in heaven give the Holy Spirit to those*
*who ask Him!" Jesus (Luke, 11:13)*

A father here on Earth, notwithstanding the blind love that often engulfs his heart, always knows how to surround his child with worthwhile gifts.

For what reason would the Celestial Father, who is all wisdom and love, remain immobile or deaf to our implorations?

The paternal devotion of the Supreme Lord surrounds us everywhere. What is of uppermost importance is that we do not poison our understanding.

We must bear in mind that Divine Providence invariably operates for the infinite well-being.

It frees the asphyxiating atmosphere with the resources of the storm.

It defends the flower with thorns.

It protects the useful plantation with disagreeable manure.

It sustains the colorful green valleys with the sturdiness of the rocks.

It is the same in the circles of planetary struggles. Occurrences that appear to us to be disastrous in our personal activity, represents support to our equilibrium, and to our success, just as phenomena that we interpret as calamities, in a collective sense, constitutes an enormous public benefit.

Pray, therefore, to the Lord for the blessing of the Divine Light for your heart and for your intelligence, so that you do not get lost in the labyrinth of problems. Nevertheless, do not forget that in the majority of the occasions, the initial assistance from Heaven reaches us through the common path, via anguish and disenchantment; but wait, confidently, as the days pass by. Time is our silent elucidater and it will reveal to your heart the infinite kindness of the Father, who will restore the health of our soul through the thorns of disillusionment or the bitter elixir of suffering.

# 64

# BETTER TO SUFFER IN RIGHTEOUSNESS

*"It is better, if it is God's will, to suffer for doing good than for doing evil." (I Peter, 3:17)*

In order to economize financial resources that he will be compelled to abandon precipitously, the human being sometimes acquires deplorable illnesses that corrode the centers of force, causing undesirable death.

By purchasing short-lived sensations for his physical body, he commonly acquires dangerous infirmities, which accompany the vehicle in which he moves about, until his last days on Earth.

By getting extremely upset over insignificant lessons on the path, he poisons vital organs, thereby creating a fatal imbalance in his physical life.

By stuffing the stomach on certain occasions, a vicious habit is established affecting important organs of the physiological instrument, thus impeding the perfect function of the carnal vessel for the simple pleasure of gluttony.

Why fear facing the obstacles of a clear path of love and wisdom if the dark road of hatred and ignorance remains replete with vengeful and disturbing forces?

How can we be afraid of fatigue and exhaustion, complications and incomprehension, conflicts and disappointments, which are the consequence of the blessed battle for the supreme victory of righteousness, when the combat for the provisional triumph of evil conduces the combatants to tributes of afflictions and sufferings?

Let us utilize our best possibilities in service to Jesus Christ by pledging our lives to Him.

The criminal weapon that breaks and the repugnant measures utilized always provoke curse and darkness; but, for the exhausted worker in his duty, and for the lamp that is extinguished in the illuminating service, a different destiny is reserved.

# 65

## LET US HAVE PEACE

*"Live in peace with each other."*
Paul (I Thessalonians, 5:13)

If it is impossible to breathe in a perfectly peaceful atmosphere among the human beings due to the ignorance and hostility so flagrant in the human path, it is logical for the apprentice to seek his inner serenity in face of the conflicts that seek to involve him constantly.

Each incarnate mind constitutes an extensive nucleus of spiritual government, subordinated at this time to just limitations, served by various powers reflected in the senses and in the perceptions.

When all of the individual centers of power are self controlled by mankind with ample movement toward legitimate righteousness, then wars shall be exiled from the Planet.

To achieve this, however, it is essential that the brothers and sisters in humanity, older in experience and in knowledge, learn to have inner peace.

To educate the vision, the hearing, the taste and the impulses, represents the primordial basis for edificating pacifism.

As a rule, we hear, we visualize and we feel according to our inclinations and not according to the essential reality. We register certain information differently from the good intentions initially based, and yes, according to our personal internal disturbance. We observe situations and scenery in the light or in the shadow that absorbs our intelligence. We perceive with the reflection or with the chaos that we install in our understanding.

This is the reason why we must, as much as possible, maintain serenity around us, as we face the conflicts encountered in the sphere in which we are situated.

Without calm it is impossible to observe and to work for righteousness.

Without inner peace, we shall never be able to reach the circles of true peace.

# 66

## GOOD WILL

*"Be very careful, then, how you live."*
*Paul (Ephesians, 5:15)*

Good will discovers work.

Work creates the renovation.

Renovation finds goodness.

Goodness reveals the spirit of service.

The spirit of service reaches understanding.

Understanding achieves humility.

Humility conquers love.

Love generates renunciation.

Renunciation reaches the light.

The light realizes self evolvement.

Self evolvement sanctifies the individual.

A sanctified individual converts the world toward God.

By walking prudently, for simple good will, the individual will reach the Divine

Kingdom of the Light.

## 67

# ILL WILL

*"Have nothing to do with the fruitless deeds of darkness."*
Paul (Ephesians, 5:11)

Ill will generates shadows.

The shadows favor stagnancy.

Stagnancy preserves evil.

Evil enthrones uselessness.

Uselessness creates discord.

Discord awakens pride.

Pride raises vanity.

Vanity stirs up inferior passions.

Inferior passions provoke lack of discipline.

Lack of discipline maintains the harshness of the heart.

Harshness of the heart imposes spiritual blindness.

Spiritual blindness leads to the precipice.

By involving himself in fruitless endeavors of incomprehension due to simple ill will, the individual can roll indefinitely toward the precipice of the shadows.

# 68

# A NECESSARY AWAKENING

*"Wake up. O sleeper, rise from the dead, and*
*Christ will shine on you."*
Paul (Ephesians, 5:14)

A great number of newcomers or not to the Christian groups, claim to have great difficulty in understanding and applying the teachings of Jesus. Some of them find obscurity in the texts, others persevere in the literary discussions. They become disturbed, they protest and reject the Divine bread for the human wrapping, which is required to preserve them on Earth.

Meanwhile, those friends do not perceive that this occurs because they remain dormant, victims of paralysis of their higher faculties.

In the majority of occasions, the Divine invitation slips by them through sanctifying suggestions; however, the distracted companions interpret them as sacred scenes, meriting praise, but very soon forgotten. The heart does not adhere remaining in a deafened sleep incapable of analyzing or understanding.

The individual needs to ask himself what he is doing, what he desires, what purpose he is seeking, and what he is aiming for. It is indispensable to self examine oneself, emerge from the animalism and stand up in order to master his own path.

Great masses, supposedly religious, are being conducted due to daily circumstances, as unconscious somnambulists. They talk about God, faith, and spirituality, as if they were breathing in a strange dark nightmarish atmosphere. Shaken up by the incessant currents of the river of life, they roll in the whirlwind of occurrences, blinded, sleepy, and half dead until they awaken and lift themselves up through their own effort, in order that Christ can enlighten them.

# 69

## TODAY

*"But encourage one another daily, as long as it is called Today, so that none of you may be hardened by sin's deceitfulness." Paul (Hebrews, 3:13)*

The suggestion regarding daily reciprocal encouragement, indicated by the Apostle Paul, requires a great deal of reflection so that we do not allow a little den of certain doubts to be created.

Let us emphasize that Paul places singular importance to time, that is called "Today," pointing out the necessity of valuing these resources along with our activity throughout the day.

Many believe that in order to give good advice to the brothers, it is necessary to communicate constantly, thus, transforming themselves into obstinate debaters. It is important to recognize, however, that a warning constituted solely of words leaves a great emptiness after they are spoken.

As occurs in the physical organizations, no spiritual edification will be constructed without foundation.

"But encourage one another" represents a more important appeal than simply calling the one involved to verbal debates.

Invitations and advice have more effectiveness when they are accompanied by the example of each one of us. All of those who live practicing the noble principles to which they devoted themselves in the world, who carefully fulfill the assumed duties and display goodness with sincerity, are leading the brothers and sisters in humanity on the uplifting path. It is for this kind of daily testimony that the Converted of Damascus invites us. Only through constant practice of inner reform will man free himself from fatal deceit.

Do not become hardened in the pathway that the Lord has led you to trek in favor of your redemption, evolvement and sanctification. Remember the importance of time that is called "Today."

# 70

## PRAISES

*"He replied: 'Blessed rather are those who hear the word of
God and obey it.'" Jesus (Luke, 11:28)*

Jesus was directing His words to the multitude, with the
enormous strength of His love, controlling the general
attention of all. He had just finished the loving and wise
observations, when a woman stood up amidst the crowd.
Magnetized by His expression of sublime spirituality, she spoke
in a loud voice about the blessings that should correspond to
Mary, for having contributed to the arrival of the Savior to
Earth. However, understanding well the unhappy consequences
that could come from this thoughtlessness expressed, the Master
responded promptly saying that prior to anything, blessed will be
those who upon hearing the revelation of God, put its teachings
into practice and observe its principles.

The passage constitutes a vivid enlightenment, not to hinder the campaign against personal praise by the sincere disciples, since it is poisonous to the most saintly tasks, suffocating its purpose and hope.

If you admire a companion that in your eyes appears to be a faithful worker for righteousness, do not perturb him with words that the world has frequently abused, repeating superficial phrases of praise but feasting dangerous flattery. Help him with goodwill and understanding in the execution of the ministry to which he was assigned, without forgetting that above all the blessings, the divine gift shines on "those who hear the words of God and obey it."

# 71

## SHAKE THE DUST OFF

> *"If anyone will not welcome you or listen to your words,*
> *shake the dust off your feet when you leave that*
> *home or town." Jesus (Matthew, 10:14)*

The disciples materialized the teaching of Jesus themselves, by shaking the dust off their sandals, and departing from this or that rebellious or impenitent place. Still, if the symbol from the Master's lesson was intended to be a simple mechanical gesture it would be merely a group of empty words

The teaching, however, is much more profound. It recommends the elimination of the sickly yeast.

To shake the dust off the feet implies the elimination of any bitterness or detritus from their lives, due to the ignorance and the perversity that is encountered on the road of our daily experiences.

It is logical to have the desire to confer to others the seeds of truth and righteousness; but, if we were received with hostility where we are visiting, it would be unreasonable to continue a long discussion and notations, that instead of being conducive to opportune success, creates shadows and difficulties around us.

If anyone did not receive your good will, nor perceive your noble intention, why waste time in bickering? Such an attitude does not resolve spiritual problems. Do you ignore the fact that the one that denies, as well as the indifferent person will also be summoned by the death of the body to our country of origin? Commend them to Jesus, lovingly, and proceed on a straight path seeking attainment of your sacred objectives. There is much to be done in the spiritual edification of the world and in you. Shake, therefore, the incorrect impressions and march ahead joyfully.

# 72

## CONTEMPLATE FARTHER AHEAD

*"For with the measure you use, it will be
measured to you." Jesus (Luke, 6:38)*

To the Eskimo, the sky is a continent made of ice, sustaining
by seals.

To the savage of the forests, there is no paradise greater
than an abundant hunt.

To a man of sectarian religious faith, the glory beyond the
grave is exclusively his and to those who love him.

To the wise man, this world and the celestial circles that
surround him are small departments of the Universe.

Transfer your observations to your field of daily
experiences and do not forget that the external situations shall
be registered within you, according to the reflections you
pictured in your conscience.

If you persevere in anger, all the forces around you will appear enraged.

If you prefer sadness you will note disenchantment in every step of the road.

If you have doubts about your personal ability, no one will have confidence in your efforts.

If you have become accustomed to habitual disturbances and difficulties, it will be next to impossible to learn to live in peace with yourself.

You will breathe in either a superior or inferior zone, tortured or peaceful, wherever you choose to direct your mind. Within the organization which pleases you, you will live with the geniuses that you call upon. If you remain idle, at rest, you will do so in whichever way you desire; if you involve yourself in work, you will find a thousand different ways of being of service.

As you stroll along, the scenery that enfolds you shall always be to your liking as you evaluate it to be, for with the same measure you apply to Nature, the living creation of God, Nature, will equally measure you.

# 73

## LET US LEARN AS QUICKLY AS POSSIBLE

*"So then, just as you received Christ Jesus as
Lord, continue to live in Him."*
Paul (Colossians, 2:6)

Among those who refer to Jesus Christ, we can identify two distinct groups: those that know Him through information received, and those who have received His benefits. The former received knowledge of the Master through books or in the exhortations of others, but marches toward the situation of the second, who have already received His blessings. To the latter the Gospel should address more emphatically.

How do we find the Lord in our journey throughout the world? Sometimes, His Divine Presence is manifested through the solution of a difficult human problem, i.e. in improved health, in the return of a loved one, in the spontaneous renovation of a path so that new illuminating light can instill better reasoning.

There are many informed people with respect to Jesus, and many have already absorbed His Saving Grace.

It is indispensable, however, that those who have received benefits from Christ, and have experienced the happiness in the blessing, also feel the same pleasure in the work and in their testimony of faith.

It will not be enough to be saturated with blessings. It is necessary that we do our part in collaborating in the service of the Gospel, attentive to its sanctifying program.

Tedious repetition and useless activities can be peculiar to spirits that are only informed; however, we who have already received the infinite Mercy of the Lord should learn, as soon as possible, to adapt ourselves to His Sublime Designs.

# 74

# BAD CONVERSATIONS

*"Do not be misled: Bad conversation
corrupts good character."*
Paul (I Corinthians, 15:33)

An undignified conversation always leaves traces of inferiority wherever it occurred. An environment of distrust immediately substitutes the climate of serenity. The poison of sick investigations disperses rapidly. After an undignified conversation, there is always less sincerity and less expression of fraternal strength. The phantoms of slander born in its dishonorable cradles and slip into good intentioned persons, intent in the destruction of honest homes; inferior preoccupations that spy from afar surge, distorting respectable attitudes; criminal curiosity emerges appearing where they have not been called, emitting distasteful opinions which induce the listeners into lies and insanity.

Bad conversation corrupts the most dignified thoughts. As a result, worthy conversations suffer, everywhere, an unstoppable persecution, thus making it crucial for Man to guard against their insistent and destructive siege.

When the heart is bestowed to Jesus, it is very easy to control situations and to eliminate dishonorable words.

Always examine the verbal suggestions that surround your daily path. Were you informed of bad news, evil accusations, and futile and malicious information regarding others? Observe your reaction. On every occasion, there are recourses to rectify lovingly, and you can renew all of this material in Jesus Christ.

# 75

# COMPLAINING

*"Do everything without complaining or arguing."*
Paul (Philippians, 2:14)

There has never been a dispute that was not preceded by inferior complaining. It is an ancient habit of frivolous people to insight ingratitude, immoral misery, pride, vanity and all the scourges that ruin souls in this world in order to organize shady conversations, where goodness, love and truth are focused with malice.

When someone starts encountering simple motives for many complaints, it is important to proceed with a rigorous self-examination in order to verify if, in fact, oneself is not suffering from the terrible illness of complaining.

Those who fulfill their duties with righteous activities will certainly not be able to have occasion for complaints.

It is indispensable for the disciple to be on guard against these accumulators of destructive energies, because in a general sense, their pernicious influence invades almost all the areas of struggle of the Planet.

It is easy to identify them. For them, everything is erroneous, nothing is good, and you can expect no better in anything. Their word is that of permanent irritability, their observations are unjust and discouraging.

Let us strive with everything within our power to counteract these humiliating mental attitudes. Confident in God, let us expand our hopes and dreams completely assured that, just as the old Proverbs assert, "an optimistic heart is the medical prescription for peace and happiness."

# 76

## THE WITNESSES

*"Therefore, since we are surrounded by such a great*
*cloud of witnesses, let us throw off everything*
*that hinders." Paul (Hebrews, 12:1)*

This concept of Paul of Tarsus should be given special consideration, by the student of the Gospel.

Each human existence is always an important day of struggle – a generous step toward the infinite ascension – and with every position taken, the individual shall always be surrounded by an enormous legion of witnesses. We are not only referring to those that form part of our own family circle, but also, above all, the friends and benefactors of each individual who observe him in the many different angles of life, from the higher spheres of the superior spirituality.

All over the world the disciple is surrounded by large clouds of spiritual witnesses that follow his every step taking note of his attitudes; because, no one accomplishes the terrestrial experience by chance without solid reasons based on love or justice.

Prior to reincarnation, generous Spirits endorsed the pleadings of the repentant soul, judges acted upon the corresponding processes, friends interceded in the service of assistance, contributing to the organization of the particulars required of the redeeming struggle. Those brothers and educators thereby become permanent witnesses of the pupil, during the length of time the new task is in progress. They speak to him without words in the innermost reaches of his conscience. Parents and children, husbands and wives, brothers and blood relatives of the world are protagonists in the evolutionary drama. The watchful observers, generally, remain on the other side of life.

Do as much good as possible toward your associates in the struggle, on this day, and do not forget those who accompany you, in spirit, truly preoccupied and lovingly.

# 77

## TO RESPOND

*"Let your conversation be always full of grace, seasoned with salt, so that you may know how to answer everyone."* Paul (Colossians, 4:6)

To respond advantageously to heterogeneous intelligence requires superior qualities that the individual should make an effort to achieve.

Not all the arguments can be directed indistinctly to the collectivity of comrades that strive among themselves in the evolving and redeeming tasks. It is necessary to refute each one with certainty. To the one that works in the country, we should not respond with references to the spectacular activities of the city. To the person that discusses the roughness of his own individual path, we should not reply with highly scientific remarks.

First of all, it is imperative not to be disagreeable to the listener, tempering the verbal attitude with legitimate comprehension of the problems in life. It would be considered as our duty to make a contribution, so that those who have deviated from simplicity and usefulness can be readjusted.

Every response in an important matter is a remedy. It is indispensable to temper the proper dose aiming at the effects. Each individual will tolerate and benefit from the proper dynamism. The very solution of truth and love in themselves should not be given without observing the same criteria. If applied in inadequate proportions, the truth could destroy, as often as, love commonly loses.

Even though you are questioned by the greatest evildoer, you should maintain a pleasant and dignified manner, in order to be clear and informative. Knowing how to respond is a virtue from the sphere of celestial wisdom. For your own good, do not forget the best method of caring for each individual.

# 78

## ACCORDING TO THE FLESH

*"For if you live according to the sinful nature,*
*you will die." Paul (Romans, 8:13)*

To the one who lives according to the flesh, that is, in conformance with the inferior impulses, the station of terrestrial struggle is no more than an empty series of events.

At each moment, limitation shall be an incessant phantom to him.

An overwhelmed brain due to negative concepts will encounter death at each step.

For the conscience that had the misfortune to hold on to such dark concepts, the human existence will not be more than a sad comedy.

Through the suffering, the cause of despair will be identified.

Through the work, destined for his spiritual purification, he feels the climate of revolt.

He will not be able to rely on the blessing of love, because, in face of his own personal appreciation, the ties of affection are simple mechanical accidents of his eventual desires.

Pain, which is the benefactor and preserver of the world, becomes intolerable to him; discipline becomes a prison of anguish, and service to others a difficult humiliation.

He is never forgiving, nor does he know how to renounce. He hates to cede to anyone, and when he is helpful he expects the servitude of a slave in return.

Wretched is the individual that lives, breathes, and acts according to the flesh. The conflicts of possession torment his heart for an indefinite length of time, with the same heat of savage life.

But "woe be unto him" because the renovating hour will always resound! If he escaped from the atmosphere of immortality, if he asphyxiated the aspiration of his own soul, if he evaded the healthy exercise of suffering, if he increased appetites and pleasures by absolute integration with the "inferior side of life," what could he expect at the end of the physical body, except the grave, shadow and impossibility into the cruel night?

# 79

## THE "BUT" AND THE DISCIPLES

*"I can do everything through Him who gives me strength."*
*Paul (Philippians, 4:13)*

The dedicated disciple affirms:

"I possess nothing of my own that is good, but Jesus will provide the resources according to my needs."

"I do not have the perfect knowledge of the road, but Jesus will guide me."

The lazy apprentice declares:

"I do not doubt the kindness of Jesus, but I do not have the strength to fulfill the Christian task."

"I know that the road remains in Jesus, but the world does not permit me to follow Him."

The first one skids the mountain of decision. He identifies his personal weaknesses; meanwhile, he is confident in the Divine Friend and deliberates in following his lessons.

The second one enjoys the rest in the valley embedded in inferior experience. He is aware of the blessings that the Master conferred to him; however, he prefers to slip away from them.

The first fixed his mind in the Divine Light and continues forward. The second halted his thoughts on his own limitations.

The "but" is the conjunction that in verbal processes usually defines our intimate position concerning the Gospel. Situated in front of the Sacred Name, it expresses firmness and confidence, faith and valor; although, when localized after it places us in indecision and uselessness, impermeability and indifference.

Only three letters denounce our route.

"Thus, my principles recommend, but Jesus asks for something else."

"It is thus that Jesus suggests, but I cannot do it."

Through one simple and small word we profess the faith or confess our inefficiency.

Remember that Paul of Tarsus, nonetheless, after being pursued and beaten, still victoriously affirmed to the Philippians:

"I can do everything through Him who gives me strength."

# 80

## THE "NO" AND THE STRUGGLE

*"Simply let your 'Yes' be 'Yes,' and your 'No,' 'No.'"*
*Jesus (Matthew, 5:37)*

Love according to the lessons of the Gospel; but, do not allow your love to become a shackle, impeding your march toward the superior life.

Be of assistance to whomsoever needs your cooperation; meanwhile, do not allow your assistance to foster disturbances and vices in another's path.

Enthusiastically assist anyone who requests a favor of you; however, do not yield to frivolity or foolishness.

Open wide the doors of well being to those surrounding you; but, do not overlook the education of your companions to true happiness.

Cultivate graciousness and cordiality; however, be loyal and sincere in your attitudes.

Saying "yes" can be very agreeable in all situations; notwithstanding, saying "no" in determined areas of human struggle, is more constructive.

Trying to satisfy all the requirements of the path is to waste time and sometimes, life itself.

Just as "yes" should be pronounced without flattery or adulation, the "no" should be pronounced without harshness.

In some instances it is necessary to contradict, so that the legitimate assistance is not lost. It is important, however, to recognize that the negative wholesome response is never a disturbance. What is disturbing is the blunt tone in which it is pronounced.

Manners for the most part, speak farther than words.

"Simply let your 'Yes' be 'Yes,' and your 'No,' 'No,'" recommends the Gospel. In order to agree or to reject, no one is obliged to be of honey or of bile. It will suffice to remember that Jesus is the Master and the Lord not only by what He does, but also, by what He does not do.

# 81

## IN PARADISE

*"Jesus answered him: I tell you the truth, today
you will be with me in paradise."*
Jesus (Luke, 23:43)

A t first glance it appears that Jesus was swayed toward the
so-called good thief, through sympathy.

But it is not so.

In the lesson of the Calvary, the Master renewed the
definition of paradise.

In another passage He, Himself, affirmed that the Divine
Kingdom does not surge with exterior appearances. It is
initiated, developed and consolidated in eternal radiance in the
intimacy of the heart.

On that hour of culminating sacrifice the good thief
unconditionally surrendered to Jesus Christ. The reader of the

Gospel is not aware of the obstinate work and the new responsibilities that would weigh on his shoulders in order to lay the foundation of his union with the Savior; notwithstanding, the reader is convinced, that, from that moment forth the former wrongdoer would penetrate the Heavens.

The symbol is beautiful and profound and gives the idea of the infinite extension of the Divine Mercy.

We can present ourselves with a voluminous baggage of debts from a dark past before the truth; but, from the instant in which we yield to the designs of the Father, sincerely accepting our obligation of individual regeneration, we advance toward a different spiritual region where "the yoke is easy and the burden is light." Upon reaching that stage, the indebted spirit will not remain in a false blessed attitude, recognizing, that above all, with Jesus, suffering is rectification and the crosses are immortal clarities.

That is the reason that the good thief, in that same hour, entered the lofty heights of paradise.

# 82

## IN SPIRIT

*"But, if by the spirit you put to death the misdeeds
of the body, you will live."*
Paul (Romans, 8:13)

He who lives according to the sublime laws of the spirit breathes in a different sphere than that of the material field in which he still places his feet.

An advanced understanding signals his intimate position.

He takes advantage of the day as the good student who is aware that his time on Earth is precious and not to be underestimated.

He discovers in the work, the blessed gift of evolving and improving.

In the ignorance of others, he discovers precious possibilities for service.

From the difficulties and afflictions on the path, he gathers resources for his own illumination and aggrandizement.

He witnesses obstacles go by, as he sees the clouds pass.

He loves responsibilities, but makes no attachments.

He directs with devotion, but does not become possessive.

He aids without unhealthy inclinations.

He serves without enslaving himself.

He is attentive to the seeding obligations; however, he does not become disquieted with the crop, because he is aware that the soil and the plant, the sun and the rain, the water and the wind, belong to the Eternal Donor.

Being the user of the Divine wealth, wherever he may be, carries with him, in his conscience and in his heart, the personal treasures.

Blessed be the individual who proceeds forth, in spirit! To him, the painful death will be no more than the dawn of a new day, a sublime transformation, and a joyous awakening.

# 83

## ACCORDING TO LOVE

*"If your brother is distressed because of what you eat, you are no longer acting in love. Do not by your eating destroy your brother for whom Christ died."*
Paul (Romans, 14:15)

In all eras dogmatic prejudices have created victims, and the heirs of Christianity were not missing in this concert of incomprehension.

Even today, the sectarian procedures, although less rigorous in their manifestations, continue to cause heartache and underestimate sentiments.

In another epoch, the disciples of Judaism provoked violent quarrels in face of the traditions regarding the impure food. Today, we no longer have the problem of carnal sacrifice at the Temple; however, new religious formalities substituted the old motifs of polemics and discord.

There are priests who only consider themselves as missionaries while performing the services that they are competent in, and believers who do not understand the meditation and the service of spiritualization except for the Sunday service, with their prayer just as an exclusive external attitude.

The disciple that has already succeeded in overcoming such barriers should cooperate in silence in order to extend the benefits of his victory.

It would be absurd to transpose the obstacle and to deliberately continue, in purely conventional demonstrations. It would be, however, lack of charity to hurl insults to the poor persons who are still undergoing mental anguish to encounter themselves, under the idea of a magnificent God.

When you observe a friend who is still prisoner of these illusions, remember that the Master also went to the cross because of him. Place kindness ahead of your analysis and your observation will be constructive and sanctifying. As long as there is understanding in the depths of your soul, you will find infinite resources for assistance, to love and to serve.

# 84

## Raising holy hands

*"I want men everywhere to lift up holy hands in*
*prayer, without anger or disputing."*
Paul (Timothy, 2:8)

In this part of the first epistle of Paul to Timothy, we receive a precious suggestion for service.

Some apprentices only desire to see an exhortation of praises in the text; notwithstanding, the converted one from Damascus, clarifies that we should raise holy hands in every place without anger or disputes.

Paul in this instance was not referring to the placing of the hands that the individual prefers to do in some religious circles where, due to the respectful artificiality of the situation, irritability or open disputes are not justifiable. The Apostle mentions the honest edification of the individual that collaborates with Divine Providence, and fulfills his daily work, which is perceived in the most hidden regions of the world.

Reading the suggestions, it is reasonable to recall that the individual in his personal effort invariably utilizes his hands in his daily work. If he is an administrator he directs the paths; if he participates in the intellectual work, he uses the pen; if he works in the field, he will drive the agriculture equipment. Paul adds that those hands should be sanctified. From that, it can be concluded that many people move their arms in their earthly task; however, it must be stressed the convenience of being aware of the intent and content of the action realized.

If you wish to apply this reasoning to yourself, pay attention before anything else if your determination is free of destructive anger and without useless demands.

# 85

# WHAT ABOUT THE ADULTERER?

*"They made her stand before the group and said to Jesus:*
*Master, this woman was caught in the*
*act of adultery." (John, 8:4)*

The case of the sinner taken by the multitude to Jesus involves significant consideration regarding the impulsiveness of man to perceive evil in others, without observing it in himself.

Amidst the reflections that the narrative suggests we can identify the erroneous concept of unilateral adultery.

If the distressed woman had been surprised in the middle of the crime, then where was the adulterer that was not brought for judgment before the populace? Would she be the only one responsible? If there was a wound in the collective group requiring intervention in order to eradicate it, in what cave was the one who had contributed to do it, hiding?

The attitude of the Master, in that hour, was characterized by infinite wisdom and inexhaustible love. Jesus could not place the weight of the blame on the unfortunate woman and allowing the perception of an overall error inquired, which of those present were without sin.

The great spontaneous silence that occurred constituted the answer more eloquently expressed than any possible verbal declaration.

Close to the adulteress also stood the perverted men who retreated in shame.

Man and woman come into the world with specific duties, which become integrated, in an essentially unique task, in the universal evolutionary plan. In the chapter regarding inferior experiences, one does not fall without the other, because both were given the same opportunity for sanctification.

If women who have deviated from the elevated mission that corresponds to them follow this sad path in society, it is because the adulterers continue to be absent in the hour of judgment, just as they had been at the time when Jesus stated His well known suggestion.

86

# To intend and to act

*"Make level paths for your feet so that the lame
may not be disabled, but rather healed."*
Paul (Hebrews, 12:13)

The well-intentioned individual will reflect intensively on
better avenues, nurturing superior ideals inclined toward
goodness and justice.

Let us agree, meanwhile, that good intentions will have
negligible results if they are not in tune with the sphere of
immediate realities, in the correct action.

It is necessary to meditate in righteousness; however, it is
crucial that we put it into practice.

Divine Providence encircles the path of the individuals
with the material for eternal edification, making possible the
construction of those "level paths" that Paul of Tarsus made

reference to. A similar accomplishment on the part of the disciple is indispensable because, pursuing his paths, the lame souls follow. The prisoners of ignorance and evil crawl as best as they can, alongside the margins of the services of superior order, and every now and then they approach the faithful servants of the Christ, proposing measures and activities in accordance with their inferior mentality. Only those who construct straight paths can escape their subtle assaults, defending themselves and also offering to them new basis, so that they will not completely deviate from the Divine Designs.

Always apply your good intentions, to the realistic practices so that your good work is illuminated with love, and your love does not become an orphan of good deeds. Accomplish this for yourself, as you need to evolve, and do it for those who seek you and who are still limping.

# 87

## ALWAIS PONDER

*"And the things you have heard me say in the presence of
many witnesses entrust to reliable men who will
also be qualified to teach others."*
Paul (II Timothy, 2:2)

The disciples of the Gospel, in Christian Spiritism, often display uncontrollable enthusiasm, anxious to extend a renewed, contagious and ardent faith. Notwithstanding, such a mental activity requires extreme caution, not only because astonishment and admiration do not signify an interior evolvement, but also, because it is indispensable to understand the spiritual qualities of the terrain to which the power of knowledge is to be transmitted.

Naturally, we are not referring to the actual dissemination of the revealing truth, nor to the manifestation of fraternal kindness, that is implied through our natural obligations in our righteous actions. We emphasize the necessity of each brother to watch over the patrimony of spiritual gifts received from the superior plane, so that the celestial values are not relegated to evil or to ignorance.

Let us spread the light of love to our companions on the journey; however, let us defend our intimate sanctuary against the thrusts of ignorance.

Let us remember that the Master Himself reserved different teachings for the popular masses and for the small community of apprentices. He did not include all the disciples in the transfiguration of the Tabor, and in the Last Supper He waited for the absence of Judas, in order to comment on the anguish that was to follow.

It is important to place attention on those attitudes of the Christ, bearing in mind that not everything is destined for all. The noble spirits that communicate on Earth always adopt a selective criterion seeking out the honorable and faithful individuals that are suited to teach others. If they, who are already able to identify problems with an illuminated vision, act prudently in that regard, how much more vigilant should be the pupil who only sees with his physical eyes? Let us work for the benefit of all, extending fraternal arms, but understanding that each person has his own step in the infinite scale of life.

# 88

## CORRECTIONS

*"Endure hardship as discipline: God is treating you as children. For what child is not disciplined by his father?" Paul (Hebrews, 12:7)*

Blessed be the spirit that comprehends the correction by the Father and accepts it graciously.

However, few individuals reach this acceptance and understanding.

At times, the generous reprimand, from on High, symbolizing a dedicated love, reaches man's campsite translating sacred and silent warnings. Nevertheless, in the majority of cases, the incarnate mind repels the saving jab and submerges into a rebellious night, thereby eliminating valuable possibilities and qualifying as an unbearable misfortune the renovating influence destined to clear up the sad dark road.

Many people facing the regenerating phenomena seek out the spectacular flight from this difficult situation and give in to a lifeless, slow suicide, abandoning themselves and becoming indifferent to their destiny.

He or she, who conducts himself or herself, in such a way, cannot be treated as a child, since he or she isolated himself or herself and fled from Divine Providence and created a compact wall of shadow between his or her own heart and the Paternal Blessings.

Those who understand the corrections from the All Merciful, readjust themselves in a new and promising circle of life.

Once the intimate tempest is overcome, they re-evaluate the opportunities of learning, serving and constructing and, based on the bitter experiences of yesterday, apply the gratitude of the superior life, looking ahead to tomorrow.

Do not forget that evil cannot offer anyone a rectification. When the correction from the Father reaches you on the path, accept it humbly, fully convinced that it constitutes a true message from Heaven.

89

# BLESSINGS

*"Blessed are you when men hate you, when they exclude
you and insult you and reject your name as evil because of
the Son of Man." Jesus (Luke, 6:22)*

The problem of the blessings requires serious reflections
before being interpreted as a resolved question in the
framework of knowledge.

Jesus confers the credential of blessed to the followers
that share with Him the afflictions and the tasks;
notwithstanding, it is important to point out that the Master
classifies sacrifices and suffering as educational and redeeming
blessings.

It is necessary then to know how to accept them.

This or that individual will be blessed for having created
goodness within material poverty, by finding happiness in

simplicity and in peace, for knowing how to maintain a long and divine hope in his heart.

However, what about the sincere adherence to the sacred obligations of the title?

The Master, in the supervision that characterizes His teachings, refers to the eternal blessings; but there are a rare few that get close to them, with that perfect understanding of one who approaches an immense treasure. The majority of the less fortunate on the terrestrial plane, upon being visited by pain, prefer the lament and despair. If they are invited to give testimony on renunciation, they slip to improper demands, and almost always, instead of working peacefully, get involved in undignified adventures in which they get lost in an uncontrolled ambition.

Jesus offered a great deal of blessings. However, only a rare few desire them. For this reason there are so many poor and many afflicted people who could be in great need in the world, but who are, as yet, not blessed by Heaven.

# 90

# THE DIVINE WORKER

> *"His winnowing fork is in his hand to clear his threshing*
> *floor and to gather the wheat into his barn, but he will*
> *burn up the chaff with unquenchable fire."*
> *John the Baptist (Luke, 3:17)*

The Apostles and the followers of the Christ from the beginning of the establishment of primitive organizations of the evangelical movement, referred to Him by diverse names.

Jesus was called Master, Pastor, Messiah, Savior and Prince of Peace. All of these titles are just and venerable; meanwhile, we cannot forget that along with these sublime invocations, came that unexpected presentation from the Baptist. The precursor designated Him as an attentive worker whose winnowing fork is in His hand to clear His threshing floor and to gather the wheat at the proper time, and who will purify the detriments with the flame of justice and of love which never goes out.

It is interesting to note that John does not introduce the Master as one imposing laws full of regulations and parchments, nor does he refer to Him according to the old Judaic traditions that awaited the Divine Messenger drawn in a carriage of magnificent glories. He refers to an optimistic, self-sacrificing worker. A rustic shovel is not lying at His side; but rather, always remains vigilant in His hands. In His spirit, reigns the hope of cleansing the Earth that was confided to His saving guidelines.

For all those who live persisting in the terrestrial services longing for a better era, maintain your heart open to the devotion to the cause of the Gospel of the Christ. Let us not be refrained by difficulties or ingratitude. Let us unfold our activities with that precious stimulus of faith, because ahead of us, blessing our humble cooperation, is that Divine worker who will clear the threshed floor of the world.

# 91

## THAT IS YOUR RESPONSABILITY

*"I have sinned. He said, for I have betrayed innocent blood. What is that to us? They replied. That's your responsibility." (Matthew, 27:4)*

Words regarding human evil are always cruel to those that listen to the criminal insinuations.

The case of Judas demonstrates the irresponsibility and the perversity of those who are involved in the execution of grave errors.

The careless spirit, upon considering the evil suggestions, in a short time is conduced to loneliness that surrounds him in the circle of disastrous consequences.

He, who conducts himself correctly, will find in the happy results of his initiatives, floods of companions who will wish to share his victories; meanwhile, rarely, will he feel the presence of someone who will share his afflictions during days of temporary defeat.

Such a reality induces one to be more cautious.

The bitter experience of Judas is still repeated daily among the majority of men, although in different fields.

There are those who listen to improper insinuations of malice or of indiscipline regarding inner tranquility referring to family matters and ordinary work. Sometimes man breathes peacefully resolving his necessary tasks; however, the envious suggestions and despair approach him, and he becomes disturbed with false hopes, inadvertently entering into dark and ingrate labyrinths. When he realizes the errors of his heart or mind, he becomes anxious toward the forerunners; however, the inferior world recalling the observations toward Judas, amusingly exclaim: "What is that to us? That's your responsibility."

# 92

## GOD DOES NOT FORSAKE YOU

*"I have given her time to repent of her
immorality, but she is unwilling."*
John (Revelations, 2:21)

Even though the Revelations is replete with profound symbols, it does not impede our examination of some expressions compatible with our understanding, withdrawing from it the appropriate lessons to amplify our spiritual progress.

The mentioned verse provides us with the understanding of the generosity of the Most High with regards to the failings and defections of His transgressing children.

Many people insist on the rigid and irrevocable determinations of divine origins; nevertheless, we must recognize that the hearts that are inclined to this interpretation, still cannot achieve and analyze the sublime essence of love that eliminates dark debts, and causes the rebirth of a new day in the horizons of the soul.

If among the judges on Earth, there exists fraternal providence, like that of conditional liberty, would the Celestial tribunal be made up of harsher and more inflexible intelligence?

The House of the Father is much more generous and magnanimous than any other known in the world, to this point, in the religious mind. In its abundant granaries there are more loans and moratoriums, concession of time and resources, than the most vigorous human imagination could conceive.

The Almighty supplies gifts to all and, nowadays, it is advisable for the earthbound individual to meditate over the resources that he was conceded by the Heavens, for his repentance, in order to readjust to the righteous paths.

The prisoners of the concept of an implacable justice ignore the tremendous intercession from the Almighty that manifests itself in a thousand different ways; however, all who seek his own personal illumination from universal love, are aware that God always provides and that it is necessary to learn how to receive.

# 93

# THE GOSPEL AND THE WOMAN

*"In this same way, husbands ought to love their wives as*
*their own bodies. He who loves his wife, loves himself."*
Paul (Ephesians, 5:28)

Many times, the Apostle of the Gentiles has been accused of severity toward women. In a number of passages in his letters to the early Christian churches, Paul proposed austere instructions which were, to some extent, shocking to many apprentices. However, few have been those able to glean from his energetic stances the mobilization of the resources of Christ in order to support the protection of women as well as her corresponding respectful qualities.

The true feminist movement actually started with Jesus. Not the movement we see today that places flags of political ideologies in the hands of feminists, but that which instills in their hearts lofty and holy directives.

During the strict religious times that preceded the arrival of Jesus, women were little more than enslaved property. Even great men such as David and Solomon did not rise above the cruelty of their time in this respect.

The Gospel, however, began a new era for women's hopes. In it we see the devotion of the Holy Mother, the sublime conversion of Mary Magdalene, the dedication of Lazarus' sisters and the faithfulness of the women of Jerusalem who followed the Lord up to the moment of His supreme sacrifice. Ever since the time of Jesus, the feminine mission became more respected on Earth. Paul of Tarsus was the consolidator of this regenerative movement. Despite the seeming harshness of his words, he sought to lift woman up from her degraded condition. Paul affirmed the right place of woman as partner of man as mother or sister, wife or daughter, and as a child of God, like himself.

# 94

## SEX

*"As one who is in the Lord Jesus, I am fully convinced that no food is unclean in itself. But if anyone regard something as unclean, then for him it is unclean." Paul (Romans, 14:14)*

When Paul of Tarsus wrote this observation to the Romans, he was referring to the nourishment that at that time created harsh discussions between the Gentiles and the Jews.

As time went by, food ceased to awaken dangerous discussions; however, we can use the argument and project it on other sectors of false opinions.

Let us refer, for instance, to sex. No other area of activity on earth suffers greater treachery. Profoundly blind of spirit the individual in general, fails to discover in it one of the most sublime motives for his existence. The most exquisite achievement in the planetary struggle as the uniting of the souls for motherhood and fatherhood, the creation and the reproduction of the forms, the extension of life, and beautiful stimulus for work and for regeneration were made possible by the Father to His children by means of the sexual emotions; however, the individuals spoil and lessen the "saintly place," populating its altars with the phantoms of excesses.

Sex established the home and created the name of mother; but, human selfishness exchanged it for absurd animalistic experiences, thereby initiating cruel trials for itself.

The Father offered a sanctuary to His sons; however, their lack of comprehension constituted an offering on their part. It is due to this that painful and distressing romances have existed in all Continents on Earth.

And still, in spite of being submerged in deplorable deviations, the individuals ask for sexual education, insisting on programs, which could be useful, but only, when the saintly notion of the divinity of the creative power is spread throughout. As long as filth still remains in the heart of he who analyzes or in the heart of he who teaches, the methods will not be other than the same lewdness.

# 95

## THIS IS THE MESSAGE

*"This is the message you heard from the beginning;*
*We should love one another." (I John, 3:11)*

All over the world we feel this tremendous anxiety to receive new messages from Heaven. Dynamic forces of the mind insist on receiving modern expressions to old truths, rehearsing varied mental creations. We notice, however, that art seeks new experiments and it becomes filled with negative images. We also notice that politics invents ideologies and processes that are unheard of in governing, and expands the course of destructive war, and that Science seeks to defer higher flights and institutes disrupting theories of well being and harmony.

Large religious orders achieve heroic work demonstrating the eternity of life, begging for spectacular signs from the invisible kingdom to the common man.

We agree that there shall always be benefit in the elevated aspirations of the human spirit, when sincerely seeking vibrations of a divine nature. However, we must realize that if there are many substantial constructive illuminating messages on Earth, the greatest and most precious of all, from the origin of the planetary organization, is the one regarding fraternal solidarity in "We should love one another."

This is the primary recommendation. By feeling it, each apprentice can examine in life's daily circle of struggle, the index of understanding that he already holds regarding the Divine Designs.

Even though this or that person has not, as yet, understood it, initiate the execution of the paternal advice within you.

Extend love always. Do good always. Start out by having esteem for those who do not understand you, convinced that they, much sooner, will do better for you.

# 96

# PRECISELY BECAUSE OF THIS

*"I do not write to you because you do not know the
truth, but because you do know it."*
*(I John, 2:21)*

The interchange, each time more intense between "the living" and "the dead," in general, constitutes a great event for the Evangelical Organizations.

It is not solely a realization for the Spiritist Organizations; it belongs to the entire Christian community.

At this time we notice that here and there, organized dogmatic protest exists; but, the revivification of the truth demands it.

Every acquisition has a price and any renovation encounters spontaneous obstacles.

The day will come when the various subdivisions of Evangelism will comprehend the divine finality of the new concert.

The movement of spiritual interchange between the two spheres widens each day. The devotion demonstrated by the discarnates provokes the attention of the incarnates.

The Lord permitted a worldwide Pentecost for the readjustment of the eternal reality.

It is worthwhile to notice that the moving and motivating voices from on High commonly reiterate formulas of the Revelation and recall the wisdom of Earth intent on extracting the most respectable concepts regarding life.

It is at this point that we remember the words of John who sincerely questioned: "Do the dead communicate with the living because individuals ignore the truth?

Not so.

If the departed once again speak to those that remain, it is because the individuals are aware of the path of Redemption with Jesus, but, they are neither inspired, nor are they encouraged to thresh out a path.

# 97

## KEEP AS PATTERN

*"What you heard from me, keep as the pattern of sound teaching." Paul (II Timothy, 1:13)*

Distribute the resources that Providence provided to your working hands; however, do not forget that the consoling words to the sickly represents a direct service from the heart in the cultivation of righteousness.

The bread from the body is alms for which you will receive proper compensation, while a friendly smile is an eternal blessing.

Send messengers to the fraternal aid; but above all, at least every now and then, do not overlook visiting the sick brother and personally listen to him.

The expedition of assistance is a gesture that will make you likeable; however, your direct intervention of assistance to the needy, will provide you with the spiritual preparation to face your own battles.

Climb the platform and teach the path of redemption to all; but interrupt your discourse, every now and then, in order to listen to the laments of a companion of human experience, even if it comes from a child of despair or of ignorance, so that you do not lose track of the proportions in your path.

Cultivate the flowers of the private garden of your loved ones, because, without the flowerbed of experience it is difficult to follow the noble and intensive cultivation of the soil; however, do not flee from the human forest, fearing the worms and monsters that inhabit it; as, it is crucial that you prepare to advance, within it, in the future.

In the circles of life, do not forget the necessity of engraving the teaching within you.

Just as it is impossible to receive individual nourishment through a substitute, or to learn a lesson, by storing it in someone else's memory, you will not be able to present yourself in front of the Supreme Forces of Wisdom and of Love, by way of victories that you have not personally lived or personally achieved.

"Keep," therefore within you "What you heard from me as the pattern of sound teaching."

# 98

## AVOID QUARRELS

*"And the Lord's servant must not quarrel."*
Paul (II Timothy, 2:24)

Avoid those who look for quarrels in the service of the Lord.

They are not in search of divine clarity for the heart. They just dispute over glory and the promotion in the area of fleeting considerations. Upon analyzing the sacred scriptures, they do not attract resources for their personal illumination, but rather, a way of putting their inferior personalism in evidence.

They combat the fellow beings that do not adopt their personal ideas, they disfavor the services that they do not hold in direct control; they do not collaborate except from the vertex to the base; they do not see advantages except in the tasks to which they themselves are assigned. They take pleasure in long discussions over where to place a comma, and they waste immense days in discovering the apparent contradictions of the writers consecrated to the ideals of Jesus. They never find time for the service of the Christian humility, simply interested in their own personal recognition. They always perceive as strange the conjugation of the verbs to help, to forgive and to serve. They invariably notice humanity's imperfection and they carry whips in their hands due to their poor taste of striking. They quarrel over all the particulars of the evangelical edification and, when the possibility for constructive agreement appears, they create new motives for disturbance.

Those that incorporate into the Redeeming Gospel, in the spirit of contention, are the greatest and most subtle adversaries of the Kingdom of God.

It is indispensable for the apprentice to be vigilant, so that he does not lose himself in the delirium of blunt useless words.

We were not called upon for quarrels, but rather, to serve and to learn with the Master; nor were we called upon to exalt the "self," but instead to fulfill the supreme designs in the construction of the Divine Kingdom within us.

# 99

## WITH ARDENT LOVE

*"Above all, love each other deeply"*
*Peter (I Peter, 4:8)*

It is not enough to proclaim virtue in favor of the establishment of the Divine Kingdom among mankind.

Problem extensively debated = solution much delayed.

Let us individually listen to the apostolic warning and swell with ardent charity, one for all.

To speak well, to teach with certainty, and to believe sincerely, are the primary phases of the service. It is crucial to work, to create and to feel with the Christ.

Fraternity simply suggested to others builds brilliant façades that experience can consume in one minute.

It is imperative to achieve the substance, the essence...

Let us be understanding with those who are ignorant, vigilant in relation to those who have gone astray in evil and in the shadows, patient toward those who are ill, serene toward the irritated, and above all, let us manifest goodwill toward all those who the Master entrusted to us for the daily teachings.

Prompt reasoning, being well prepared to act with agility on Earth, can constitute a valuable patrimony; on the other hand, if the heart is lacking in feeling for the problems, in conducting and resolving them for the common good, he will be susceptible to being easily converted into a calculator.

Let us not be detained in theoretic compassion.

Let us seek fraternal love, spontaneous, ardent and pure.

Heavenly charity not only scatters benefits, it also radiates the Divine Light.

# 100

## LET US GIVE THANKS

*"Give thanks in all circumstances, for this is
God's will for you in Christ Jesus."*
Paul (I Thessalonians, 5:18)

The stone secures.

The thorn alerts.

Bile remedies.

Fire recasts.

Garbage fertilizes.

Storms purify the atmosphere.

Suffering redeems.

Illness alerts.

Sacrifice enriches life.

Death always renovates.

Let us learn, therefore, to praise the Lord for the blessings He bestows upon us.

Good is the heat that modifies; good is the cold that preserves.

The happiness that stimulates is the sister to the pain that perfects us.

Let us pray to Heavenly Providence for enough light, so that our eyes may be able to identify the granary of grace in which we find ourselves.

It is our inner blindness that causes us to trip over obstacles, wherein only divine favor exists.

And, especially upon announcing a noble wish, let us prepare ourselves to receive the lessons, which we should take advantage of, in order to achieve it according to the superior goal that directs our destiny.

Let us not be frightened by difficulties or unforeseen suffering.

Not always does the assistance from on High appear in the form of a celestial delicacy.

Quite often it appears in the form of an undesired recourse. Let us remember that an individual in danger of drowning in the deep waters that cover the abyss sometimes succeeds in being saved at the price of hard knocks.

Let us give thanks, therefore, for all the experiences of the evolutionary path, in the sanctifying search of the Divine Will, in Jesus Christ, our Lord.

# 101

## RESIST TEMPTATION

*"Blessed is the man who perseveres under trial"*
*(James, 1:12)*

While our spiritual ship navigates through the waters of inferiority, we cannot maintain immunity from harsh interior conflicts. Primarily in the corporeal sphere, every time that we intend the improvement of the soul, making use of the work and obstacles in the world, we should be on the look-out for the multiplication of the difficulties that we come across, right in the middle of the road of illuminated knowledge.

In opposition to our great desire for clarification, there are thousands of millenniums of shadows. Interfering with our most humble aspiration for advancement in righteousness, there were centuries in which we took pleasure in evil.

For this reason, in spite of the blessings from on High, so many temptations exist on the path of the disciples.

Sometimes the apprentice feels he is well prepared to overcome the beastly dragons that surround his doors; however, when he least expects it, the degrading suggestions pry upon him, obliging him once again to engage in a difficult battle.

Therefore, it is apparent that not even the grave exonerates us from the obstacles with the shadows, whose roots extend into our spiritual organization. Only the death of the imperfection within each one of us, will liberate us from it.

Let there be constructive tolerance surrounding human advancement, as the evil insinuations will surround us everywhere, while we delay in the partial achievement of righteousness.

We shall only achieve liberation when we obtain complete light.

Fully understanding the importance of the matter, the Apostle proclaimed, "Blessed is the man who perseveres under trial." At the present time it is impossible to reach any reference of absolute triumph, as we are still so far apart from an angelic state. Nevertheless, blessed shall we be if we go through these types of battles, controlling the impulses of our least advanced sentiments, thereby, perfecting it, little by little, through our personal efforts, so that we do not lifelessly give in to the inferior suggestions that seek to convert us into living instruments of evil.

# 102

## CAESAR AND US

> *"Then Jesus said to them: Give to Caesar what is Caesar's and to God what is God's."*
> *(Mark, 12:17)*

Everywhere in the world the individual will encounter according to his personal merits, the figure of Caesar symbolized in the state government.

Evil men will, no doubt, produce evil statesmen.

Idle and indifferent groups will receive disorganized administrations.

In any case, the influence of Caesar will surround the individual, demanding the fulfillment of the material commitments.

It is imperative to give him what is his.

The student of the Gospel should not invoke religious principles or individual idealism, in order to escape from these obligations.

If there are errors in the laws, remember the extent of our individual debts with the Divine Providence, and let us collaborate with the human governing body, by offering our participation in the task and our good will, conscientiously aware that our disinterest or rebelliousness will not resolve our problems.

It is preferable for the disciple to sacrifice himself, go through suffering, than delaying his advancement while upholding respectable laws that direct him, transitorily, in the physical plane, whether it be through indiscipline in following the established principles or due to excessive enthusiasm that could tempt him to advance too rapidly at the time.

Are there iniquitous decrees?

Remember and see if you have already cooperated with those who govern the material world.

Live in harmony with your superiors, and do not forget that the best position to maintain is that of equilibrium.

If you intend to live correctly, do not direct the harsh bitter vinegar of your criticism to Caesar. Assist him with your capable efficiency and sensible desire to act correctly, fully convinced that he and we are children of the same God.

# 103

## THE CROSS AND AND DISCIPLINE

> "A certain man from Cyrene, Simon, the father of
> Alexander and Rufus, was passing by on his
> way and they forced him to carry the cross."
> (Mark, 15:21)

Many students of Christianity disagree with the documented history on the cross, alleging that the reminiscences of the Calvary constitutes improper culture of the suffering.

They affirm that the memory of the Master in those last hours of the crucifixion, amidst vulgar evildoers is a negative one.

But, we are of those who prefer to visualize every day in the life of Jesus as a glorious journey, and all of the minutes as divine parcels from His sacred ministry, ahead of the necessities of the human soul.

Every hour of His presence among the people is characterized in a particular beauty, and the instant of the shameful cross is replete of majestic symbolism.

Various disciples weave extensive tales regarding the cross of the Lord and they usually examine with theoretical particulars the imaginary logs they carry along with them.

However, only the one who has actually shouldered the cross of redemption that is his responsibility, is the one who has achieved the strength of denying himself, in order to follow in the footsteps of the Divine Master.

Many persons confuse discipline with spiritual illumination. Only after having accepted the gentle yoke of Jesus Christ, will we be able to raise the cross to the shoulders, which will concede us the spiritual wings for eternal life.

Against the arguments, which are usually useless, of those who did not truly comprehend the sublimity of the cross, let us observe the example of the man from Cyrene in those culminating moments of the Savior. The cross of the Christ was the most beautiful in the world; nonetheless, the individual that assists Him, does not do so of his own volition, but rather, adhering to an irresistible requirement. And, even today, the majority of individuals accept the obligations inherent to their duty, because to this they feel obliged.

# 104

# A SACRED RIGHT

*"For it has been granted to you, on behalf of Christ not
only to believe in Him, but also to suffer for Him."*
*Paul (Philippians, 1:29)*

To cooperate personally with the human administrators in a direct sense, has always been the object of ambition of the workers of this or that terrestrial organization.

It is an act of true confidence to be able to share the responsibilities between the superior who knows how to be just, with the subordinate who knows how to serve. It establishes the basis for harmony in the daily activities, a realization that all institutions seek to attain.

Many of the students of Christianity appear to ignore that with regards to Jesus the reciprocity is the same, elevated to the maximum degree, in the area of fidelity and comprehension.

A greater understanding of the divine program signifies, a greater expression of individual testimony in the services of the Master.

Expanded competence – greater accumulation of duties.

The more light – the more vision.

Many individuals who have naturally achieved certain intellectual characteristics, but still considered mentally sick, would like to accept the Savior and believe Him, but, they cannot instantly achieve such an inner personal evolvement. Because of the ignorance they fail to eliminate and the capriciousness they possess, they fail to integrate in the right to perceive the Truths of Jesus. This will only be achieved when they readjust, which is indispensable.

However, the disciple who has achieved the benefits of the faith was considered worthy of residing spiritually with the Master. Between he and the Lord, an exchange of confidence and of responsibility does already exist. Nevertheless, while persevering in the joys of Bethlehem and the glories of Capernaum, the labor of faith unfolds marvelously; but, in occurring the division of the anguish of the cross, many apprentices flee fearing the suffering, revealing themselves unworthy of being selected. Those who behave like this are categorized as crazy, as, to withdraw from collaborating with Christ, is to scorn a sacred right.

# 105

## THE MOST IMPORTANT OBSERVATION

*"The most important one, answered Jesus, is this:*
*Hear, O Israel, the Lord our God, the Lord is one."*
*(Mark, 12:29)*

On replying to the scribe that had interrogated him, with regards to the most important of all the commandments, Jesus preceded the initial article of the Decalogue with an observation that merits pointing out.

Prior to any of the programs of Moses, the Revelations of the Prophets and of his own redeeming Blessings in the Gospel, the Master chooses an energetic declaration of principles, proclaiming all the spirits to a plane of substantial unity. Basing the services of salvation that He solely had brought from the higher spheres, Jesus Christ proclaimed to all of humanity that only one Almighty God exists, the Father of Infinite Mercy.

He was aware, in advance, that many men would not accept the truth, that many souls would make an effort to escape from their just obligations, that there would be delays, ill will, indifference and laziness regarding the Glad Tidings. Nonetheless, He sustained divine unity, in order that the apprentices would become convinced that they could poison their own liberty, create fictitious Gods, raise discord and temporarily betray the Law, station themselves on the roads, attempt war and destruction. In spite of this, they would never be able to fool the plan of the eternal truths, to which all will become adjusted one fine day, to the perfect understanding that the Lord is our God, the Lord is one.

# 106

## THERE IS A GREAT DIFERENCE

*"Then Peter said, silver or gold I do not have,*
*but what I have I give you."*
*(Acts, 3:6)*

It is justifiable to recommend caution to those who are interested in the advantages of human politics, reporting to Jesus, while trying to explain via the Gospel, about certain absurdities existing in social theories.

Usually man made Laws directing individuals addresses the governed, using this format: "Whatever you own, belongs to me."

In Christianity, meanwhile, the inspired lips of the Apostle Peter assures the ears of all: "What I have, that, I give to you."

Have you meditated over the greatness of the world, when men would be resolved to give that which they possess for the edification of Universal evolution?

In common charitable services, in the institution of public charities, seldom does the individual cede to his fellow man, that which constitutes his own intrinsic property.

In genuine service for the eternal good of all, will there be someone who totally entrusts his perishable earthly goods?

A generous individual will distribute money and useful things with the needy on the path; notwithstanding, he will not register within him the light and happiness that are born from those offerings, if he did not realize these actions with a sentiment of love, which at the root lays his legitimate eternal wealth.

Each individuality brings forth with them the noble qualities that they have already mastered and with which they will always be able to advance in the area of spiritual acquisitions, of a higher superior order.

Do not forget the loving words of Peter and give of yourself in an effort toward salvation, because, he who is waiting for gold or silver to contribute to good deeds, truly will find himself far from the possibility of helping himself.

# 107

## COMPASSION

> *"But compassion with contentment is great gain."*
> *Paul (I Timothy, 6:6)*

Much is spoken on Earth about compassion, however, when we refer to this virtue, it is difficult for us to discern between compassion and humiliation.

"I help, but this individual is given to vice."

"I will assist, but this woman is ignorant and evil."

"It saddens me, however, that person is an ingrate and cruel."

"I feel compassion, but it involves a useless person."

Such affirmations are repeated often from lips that affirm to be Christian.

Truly, in general, we only encounter on Earth that compassion of soft voice and thorny hands.

It spreads honey and poison.

It places a balsam on the wounds as it rips them open.

It extends open arms and collects on debts of recognition.

It rescues and beats.

It protects but does not stimulate.

It offers kind words yet thrusts hostile retorts.

It appeases the hunger of the travelers in the terrestrial experience with bread full of bile.

The true compassion, however, is the legitimate daughter of love.

It wastes no time in stressing evil.

It is solely concerned with goodness instead of wasting effort with childishness and is aware that time is precious in life.

The Gospel does not refer to that false pity, full of illusions and demands. He, who reveals the sufficient energy to embrace a Christian life, finds the resources to assist happily. He does not become tied down to destructive criticism, and knows how to plant goodwill, fortify the seeds, cultivate the sprouts and await the production.

Paul says: "But compassion with contentment is great gain" for the soul, and truly we know of no other that could bring more prosperity to the heart.

# 108

# PRAYER

*"Devote yourself to prayer, being watchful and thankful."*
*Paul (Colossians, 4:2)*

Many believers would like to use the prayer as if they were mobilizing a broom or a hammer.

They expect immediate results, without being aware of any prior preparatory effort. Others persevere in the repetition of the prayer while frightened and in anguish. They waste effort and consume valuable energy in unjustifiable affliction. They visualize only the evil and the shadows, and never take the time to examine the tender young sprout of the Divine seed or the close or remote possibility of goodness. They incarcerate themselves on the "wrong side" and, sometimes, lose an entire existence without the effort of transferring themselves to the "right side."

What probability of success could be provided to the needy one that shouts out a prayer with evident symptoms of an imbalance? A prudent concessionary, to begin with, would delay the solution, prudently awaiting serenity to return to the petitioner.

The words of Paul in this sense are clear.

"Devote yourself to prayer, being watchful and thankful." It is imperative to recognize that to praise is not solely the utterance of beautiful expressions; it is also to be happy, while in actual combat for the victory of goodness, expressing gratitude to God for the motive of the suffering and sacrifice, seeking to find the advantages that adversity and the efforts brought to the spirit.

Let us ask Jesus for the gift of peace and happiness; but let us not overlook glorifying the supreme designs, each time that His merciful and Just Will clashes with our inferior objectives. Let us be convinced that a prayer contrived of desperate thoughts and inopportune demands is destined to the renovating floor as occurs to an unproductive flower that the winds blow away.

# 109

## THE THERE IMPERATIVES

> *"So I say to you: Ask and it will be given to you; seek and*
> *you will find; knock and the door will be opened to you."*
> Jesus (Luke, 11:9)

Ask, seek, and knock.

These three imperatives of the recommendations of Jesus were not pronounced without a special significance.

In the entangled struggles and debts in the terrestrial experience, it is crucial that the individual learns to ask for the paths of liberation from old conventional suffocating chains, sterile preconceptions, and empty old habits. It is necessary to forcefully and decisively desire to come out of that dark brush in which the majority of individuals lose sight of the eternal interests.

Immediately thereafter, it is imperative to seek.

The procurement consists of selective efforts. The field is replete with inferior attractions, some of which are full of brilliant suggestions. It is indispensable to locate the dignified sanctifying action. Many seek dangerous mirages somewhat like that of the butterfly that becomes fascinated with the brightness of a fire. They approach from afar, and get close to the flames, which consumes the blessing of their body.

It is imperative to learn to seek out legitimate goodness.

Once the sanctifying path is established, the moment has arrived to knock on the door of edification; but, without hammering methodically and without the chisel of good will, it is extremely difficult to transform the resources of the corporeal life into luminous works of divine art, when looking ahead to spiritual happiness and eternal love.

It will matter little to pray without direction, to procure without examination, and to act without an elevated objective.

Let us plead with the Father for our liberation from primitive animalism. Let us seek the sublime spirituality and work to localize ourselves within it, in order to become converted into faithful instruments of the Divine Will.

Ask, Seek, and Knock!... This trilogy of Jesus enfolds a special significance for the students of the Gospel in all epochs.

# 110

## PERSONAL MAGNETISM

*"And the people all tried to touch him, because power*
*was coming from him and healing them all."*
*(Luke, 6:19)*

In actuality today, we observe a Pleiades of eminent spiritualists spreading various concepts relative to personal magnetism, with great astonishment, as if we were actually experiencing a novelty of the nineteenth century.

This service of investigation and dissemination of the occult powers of individuals represents a valuable contest in the work of the present and future education; however, it is important to recall that the edification is not new.

Jesus, in His passage through this planet, represented individualized sublimity of personal magnetism, in His expression substantially Divine. Individuals would dispute over His enchanting presence, the multitude would follow His steps, touched with unique admiration. Almost all the people wanted to touch His clothing. Radiations of love emanated from Him, which would neutralize recalcitrant illnesses. The Master spontaneously produced a climate of peace, which would reach anyone who enjoyed His presence.

If you are seeking an easier path for the true blossoming of your psychic potential, it is logical, therefore, to take advantage of the experience that the earthly instructors offer you, in that sense; but, do not forget the examples and the vivid demonstrations of Jesus.

If you intend to attract, it is imperative, first, to know how to love. If you desire to achieve legitimate influence on Earth, sanctify yourself through the influence of Heaven.

# 111

## WIN FRIENDS

*"I tell you, use worldly wealth to gain friends for yourselves." Jesus (Luke, 16:9)*

If the individual could succeed in discovering through human experience the profound past, he would more rapidly reach the conclusion that all the opportunities that complement him in knowledge and health come from Divine Kindness, and that most of the material resources that are at his disposition and desires proceed from injustice.

It is not up to us to particularize, but rather to deduce that the concepts of human rights originated from the divine influence because, as far as we are concerned, we are compelled to recognize our slow individual evolution from fierce selfishness toward a universal love, from the iniquity toward true justice.

It will be enough to recall in this sense that almost all the Countries arose, centuries ago, through cruel conquests. With exception, men have been squandering servants that at the moment of adjustment did not appear to be worthy of the benefits received.

It is for this reason that Jesus left us the parable of the unfaithful servant, inviting us into a sincere fraternity in order that through it we could find the path of rehabilitation.

The Master encouraged us to gain friends, that is, to expand our circle of friends through which we can feel more intensive protection in a spirit of cooperation and through intervening values.

If our spiritual past is somber and painful, let us try to simplify it, by acquiring true dedications that will assist us through the harsh climb of redemption. If we do not, today, have a determined bond with the wealth of injustice, we had it yesterday, and it becomes indispensable that we take advantage of time for our own individual readjustment before the Divine Justice.

# 112

## ETERNAL TABERNACLES

> *"I tell you, use worldly wealth to gain friends for*
> *yourselves, so that when it is gone, you will be*
> *welcomed into eternal dwellings"*
> Jesus (Luke, 16:9)

An individual unaware of his spiritual obligations will consider that he finds in this passage an intelligent thief buying the favors of mercenary attorneys in order to reintegrate in the honorable titles of human convention. However, when Jesus spoke of friends, he was referring to sincere and consecrated brothers; when He referred to the riches of injustice, He was including the total past life of the individual, involving all of the painful lessons that characterize it. In the same manner, when He referred to the eternal tabernacles, he did not place them on a celestial stage.

The Master situated the sacred tabernacle in the heart of man.

More than anyone, the Savior identified our imperfections, and viewing us with immense pity, due to the deficiencies existing in our spirits, He uttered the divine words that will be helpful for our studies.

Being cognizant of our errors He affirmed, in essence, that we should take advantage of the transitory riches at our reach, actively involving us in the legitimate fraternity, in order that, by forgetting our crimes and hatred of other times, we become true brothers, one with the other.

Let us evaluate in this manner the permanence of our service on Earth, while incarnates or as discarnates, favoring all the resources at our disposal, the personal improvement and the elevation of our fellow man, participating in the direction of the light and always loving. By living within these norms of sublime solidarity, we will always be able to count on the dedication of faithful friends, who, being dedicated disciples more noble than we, will be able to assist us effectively by taking us into their hearts, converted in tabernacles of the Lord. They will assist us not only to obtain new opportunities of readjustment and sanctification, but also by endorsing our promises and aspirations before Jesus, regarding the superior life.

# 113

## YOUR FAITH

*"Then He said to her: Daughter, your faith has healed you. Go in peace." Jesus (Luke, 8:48)*

It is important to observe that the Divine Messenger, after having dispensed beneficial assistance, always made a reference to the marvel of faith, which is a sublime patrimony to those who seek Him.

On diverse occasions we heard His expressive affirmation: "Your faith has healed you." The sick in body and in the soul, after their improvement or through their cure would hear that noble phrase. It is that the will and the confidence of men are powerful factors in the development and illumination of life.

The navigator without a course and without faith, will only be able to reach port, by virtue of the movement of forces in which he balances; however, absolutely ignoring what could occur to him.

The patient, who is incredulous of the action of the remedies, is the first to work against his own security. The man that appears to be disenchanted with everything will not respond with any useful cooperation in anything.

The souls that are empty, in vain claim the happiness that they feel the world owes them. The denials through which they wander, in life they transform into deadening zones, as isolators of electricity. Vitalizing current goes through, however, they appear insensitive.

In the enterprises and necessities on your path, do not isolate yourself in negative positions. Jesus can overcome all, your true friends will do anything possible for you; in spite of this, neither the Master nor your companions will be able to provide you, in an integral sense, that happiness that you seek, without the assistance of your faith, because you are also a child of the same God, with the identical possibilities of elevation.

# 114

## THE NEW ATHENIANS

*"When they heard about the resurrection of the dead, some
of them sneered, but others said: we want to hear you
again on this subject." (Acts, 17:32)*

The contact that Paul had with the Athenians in Areopagus
represents a very interesting lesson for the new disciple.

While the Apostle commented on his impressions of the
well-known city, possibly foretelling the vanity of those present
as he made references to the sanctuaries, and because of the
subtle fire of reasoning, he was heard attentively. It is possible
that the assembly would have acclaimed him with fervor, if his
reference had remained philosophical as in the first expositions.
Athens would revere him, as a wise man, presenting him to the
world in the special mold of its other unforgettable names.

Paul however, makes references to the resurrection of the
dead introducing the glorious continuation of life, beyond the

trivialities of Earth. From that moment on, the audience started to feel uncomfortable and mocked his beautiful, sincere words, departing and leaving him practically alone.

The teaching encompasses perfectly well on the continuing days of today. Numerous members of the group of workers for the Christ, in the diverse sectors of the modern culture, are attentively heard and respected for their authority in the subject matter that they specialized in; however, when they openly declare their belief in a life beyond the physical body, reiterating the law of responsibility far beyond the sepulcher, they immediately receive sarcastic mocking from these original admirers, leaving them alone, giving the impression of a true desert.

# 115

## THE DOOR

*"Therefore Jesus said again: I tell you the truth. I am the gate for the sheep." (John, 10:7)*

It is not enough to achieve the qualities of the sheep, with regards to its gentleness and tenderness in order to reach the Divine Kingdom.

It is necessary for the sheep to recognize the door of redemption with the indispensable discernment and guard the path, disregarding the pleas of an inferior order that appear from the edges of the road.

From this we can conclude that the gentleness that is needed to be victorious, does not exempt one from the caution in the orientation to follow.

Not always, the loss of the herd comes from the attack by beasts; but rather, because the inattentive sheep transpose the natural barriers, deaf to the voice of the shepherds and blind to the appropriate exits, searching for the pastures to follow. How many are attacked unexpectedly by the terrible wolf, because, fascinated by neighboring green pastures they deviate from their own road, overcoming obstacles, in order to attend to destructive impulses.

That is what occurs to individuals in the course of their experience.

How many noble spirits have lost precious opportunities due to their own indiscretion? Some men of admirable patrimony sometimes become arbitrary and capricious. In the majority of the situations, they imitate the virtuous and useful sheep who, after having achieved various ennobling titles, forgets the door to be reached and breaks the necessary and beneficial discipline in order to yield to the devouring wolf.

# 116

## LISTEN TO THEM

*"Abraham replied: They have Moses and the Prophets; let them listen to them." Jesus (Luke, 16:29)*

The response given by Abraham in the parable to the wealthy man is still a valuable teaching for our daily life on the ordinary path.

Innumerable people approach the fountains of spiritual revelation, but have not achieved their liberation from their selfish ties in a way that will allow them to see and to listen, as needed, for their essential interests.

It has been precisely a century since the establishment of a more extensive interchange between the two planes through the great movement of the revived Christianity; notwithstanding, there are apprentices who contemplate the Heavens unhappily distressed over not having received a personal message directly from a father or a son in their human experience. Some erroneously deviate from the path, alleging such motives. To these, the phenomenon and revelation in Evangelical Spiritism are simply lies as they have not received anything from relatives that had passed away, during consecutive years of observation.

That is nothing but a mere contradiction.

Who can guarantee the perpetuity of those fragile threads in the terrestrial ties?

The animal impulse has limits.

Let no one justify, his own blindness due to the dissatisfaction of a personal whim.

The world has been replete with messages and emissaries for thousands of years. Notwithstanding, the great problem does not lie in demanding the truth in order to attend the exclusive circle of each person, but rather, in the consideration by each individual with regards to the forward march ahead in his own valor toward the direction of the eternal realities.

# 117

## IN THE FAMILY

*"These should learn, first of all, to put their religion*
*into practice by caring for their own family and*
*so repaying their parents and grandparents,*
*for this is pleasing to God."*
Paul (I Timothy, 5:4)

The struggle in the family is a fundamental problem in the redemption of human beings on Earth. How can we be the benefactors to one hundred or one thousand people, if we have not, as yet, learned to serve five or ten individuals? This is a logical question, which extends to all sincere disciples of Christianity.

A good speaker and a bad servant are two titles that cannot be mixed.

The Apostle recommends the exercise of observing compassion in the center of all domestic activities. He does not allude to the compassion that weeps without courage when faced with afflictive enigmas, but rather, the one that recognizes the neuralgic zones of the home and strives to eliminate them, mindful of the Divine decisions, at the propitious time.

We know numerous brothers who feel spiritually lonely among those who have entered into their personal family circle through family blood ties, thereby falling into lamentable discouragement.

It is crucial, however, to examine these transitory physical bonds cognizant that there are no casual unions in existence on Earth, in a family household. Meanwhile, there is a preponderance of renovating and regenerating trials prevailing there. Therefore, let no one fail to take advantage of this sacred field of opportunity to be of service, even though you feel oppressed or overwhelmed by the incomprehension. It will constitute a grave error to overlook the infinite possibilities for illuminating service.

It is impossible to try to help the entire world when we fail to be useful in a small home, the one, in which the Will of the Father situated us, on a temporary basis.

Prior to making a great personal projection into collective service, let the student learn to cooperate in behalf of his family members of today, convinced that such an effort represents an essential achievement.

# 118

## FOR THIS REASON

*"Do not repay evil with evil or insult with insult, but with blessing, because to this you were called so that you may inherit a blessing." (I Peter, 3:9)*

The line of the complainers has always been numerous in all tasks of goodness.

In the evangelical apostolate we equally observe this general rule.

Many apprentices, obedient to the pernicious habit, prefer the path of strife or of scandalous dissent. However, some additional reasoning might awaken the community of the students for greater comprehension.

Would Jesus invite us to sterile conflicts only to repeat scenes of individual whims or of a tyrannical force? If such were the case, the Ministry of the Kingdom would be entrusted to the obstinate, to the debaters or to the giants of physical energy.

It would be senseless for the server of the Glad Tidings to be involved in laments that have no reason for being.

Bitterness, persecution, slander, brutality, lack of understanding, are ancient factors that torment the souls on Earth. In order to contribute to their extinction, is the reason that the Lord called us to the task. Do not foster them by paying too much attention to them.

The Christian is the live point of resistance to evil, wherever it may be.

Think about this and seek to comprehend the significance of the verb "to withstand."

Do not forget your obligation to serve with Jesus.

It is for this purpose that we were called.

# 119

## ALWAYS BE OF ASSISTANCE

*"Then Paul answered: Why are you weeping and breaking my heart?" (Acts, 21:13)*

It constitutes one of the most dramatic passages in the Acts of the Apostles the one in which Paul of Tarsus is preparing to confront the testimonies that awaited him in Jerusalem.

In the heroic soul of the fighter, not a shadow of hesitation exists. His spirit, as usual, is ready. But his companions are crying and lamenting, and from the sensitive valiant heart of the warrior of the Gospel flows his painful question.

In spite of the serene energy, that controlled his vigorous organization, Paul felt the lack of courageous friends like himself.

The companions that were following him were sincerely ready for the sacrifice; however, they did not know how to manifest the sentiments of a faithful soul. It is because the crying and lamenting have never helped in difficult moments. Whomsoever cries, around a friend in a precarious position, disorganizes such friend's resistance.

Jesus shed tears in the Garden of Olives when He was alone, but in Jerusalem, under the weight of the cross, He begged the kind ladies, who help Him, to eliminate their painful tears. On the dawn of the Resurrection, He asks Magdalene to clarify the motive for her tears at the gravesite.

This lesson is of great significance for all students.

If a beloved soul is caught in a tempest for a long time, do not fall into useless desperation. The complaints do not resolve problems. Instead of tears and laments, get close to him and extend your arms.

# 120

## CONCILIATION

*"Settle matters quickly with your adversary who is taking*
*you to court. Do it while you are still with him on*
*the way, or he may hand you over to the judge,*
*and the judge may hand you over to the officer,*
*and you may be thrown into prison."*
Jesus (Matthew, 5:25)

Many ennobled souls, after having received the exhortation from this passage, intimately suffer after stumbling across their former adversary of yesterday, who is inaccessible to any conciliation.

The advice of the Master, notwithstanding, is a fundamental consolation to the individual conscience.

Assert the words of the Master – "Settle matters" which is the equivalent of saying "do your part."

Correct whatever you can with regards to errors of the past; mobilize every effort to display your goodwill with perseverance. Insist on kindness and in comprehension.

If the adversary is ignorant, meditate over the time in which you too were unaware of your primordial obligations, and observe if you as well did not act with worse characteristics. If he is perverse, classify him among the sick and demented on the road to being cured.

Do as much good as possible as long as you are walking on the same road; because if the enemy is so implacable, that he seeks you in order to turn you over to the judge, you will also have proof and testimonies to present. A legitimate trial includes all the pieces, and only the spirits that frankly are impenetrable to righteousness will undergo the rigors of the extreme justice.

Always strive, as much as possible, for harmony; but, if the adversary scorns your good efforts, settle matters yourself with your own conscience and wait confidently.

# 121

## MANURE PILE

*"It is fit neither for the soil nor for the manure pile; it is thrown out. He who has ears to hear let him hear."*
Jesus (Luke, 14:35)

As we can deduce it, Jesus paid significant attention to the manure pile.

Soil and fertilizer in this passage are given essential importance. With the first we will achieve the planting, with the second it is possible to make the fertilizer, wherever it is necessary.

A great number of apprentices by imitating the actions of the former Pharisees flee from the first encounter with the "manure zones" of others; meanwhile, this happens because they are unaware of their useful expressions.

The Gospel is full of lessons in that area of illuminating knowledge.

If Joseph of Galilee or Mary of Nazareth symbolized lands full of virtue, the same does not occur to the Apostles who have to revert, at each step, to the fountain of tears arising from the manure piles of remorse and human weaknesses, in order to fertilize the impoverished soil of their hearts. How much fertilizer of this nature did Magdalene and Paul need to accumulate before achieving the glorious position in which they became so outstanding?

Let us transform our miseries into lessons.

Let us identify the manure that our own ignorance piled up because of our own selves and convert it into fertilizer in our intimate soil; and we will have reasonably resolved the problem of our greatest ills.

# 122

# SIN AND SINNER

*"Beloved, do not imitate what is evil, but what is good.*
*He who does good is of God, but he who does evil*
*has not seen God." (III John, 11)*

The human society should not try to divide itself, as if it were a camp in which the "good" and the "evil" are separated; but rather, should live like a large family in which the spirits that have come to understand the Father, and those who have not, as yet, been able to sense Him become integrated.

Of course, the words "evil" and "perversity" will continue to exist for a vast number of years in the Earth's dictionary defining certain inferior mental attitudes; however, it is important to understand that the question of evil has been receiving newer interpretations in human intelligence.

The evangelist presents a just concept. John does not say that the perverse one is exiled from our Father, nor that he remains absent from the Creation. He merely affirms that he "has not seen God."

This does not mean that we should cross our arms before the poisoned grasses and pestilent zones on the road; however, it obliges us to remember that the worker does not retrieve the thorns and residues from the soil, to convert it into precipices.

Many people think that the "fallen man" is one who should be annihilated. Jesus, however, did not adopt this norm. Upon directing Himself lovingly to the sinner, it was obvious He was facing a sick unhappy person, from whom the caracteristics of eternity could not be withdrawn.

Fight crime, but protect the individual that becomes involved in its dark shadowy net.

The Master indicated the constant battle against evil, however, He recognizes a legitimate fraternity between men as a sublime landmark of the Celestial Kingdom.

# 123

## COMMON CONDITION

*"Immediately the boy's father exclaimed: I do believe;*
*help me overcome my unbelief."*
*(Mark, 9:24)*

That individual that approached Jesus from the multitude, holding his sick son in his arms, constitutes the common spiritual expression of humanity on Earth.

The religious circles comment excessively on their faith in God; however, during stormy moments, there are few devotees that maintain this firm confidence.

The masses reveal themselves to be very attentive to the ceremonies of the exterior worship, participating in the evolvement of their faith; but, when confronted with scandalous difficulties, almost everyone slips on the cliff of reciprocal accusations.

If a missionary fails, the abandonment is verified. The community of believers keeps their eyes on the fallible men being blind to the ultimate goal or indifferent to the institutions. In a movement of such spiritual insecurity, without paradox, human beings believe and disbelieve, having confidence one day and lacking it the next.

We are still confronted by the uncertainties of immature spirits, who have only commenced to conceive the notions of responsibility.

Happy are those who alike the needy father, get close to the Christ, confessing their precarious intimate position. Thereby, affirming their faith verbally, they will at the same time plead for assistance for their lack of faith, tearfully attesting to their own miserable position.

# 124

## NOT LACKING

*"If I send them home hungry, they will collapse on the way, because some of them have come a long distance." Jesus (Mark, 8:3)*

The preoccupation that Jesus had for the multitudes continues alive through time.

How many religious faiths palpitate in the hearts of the Nations influenced by the providential love of the Divine Master?

There may be some perverse, desperate men, who persevere in evil and in denial, but a community cannot be seen without the help of faith. Even the savages receive positions of assistance from the Father, naturally, according to their rustic primitive interpretations. Food from Heaven is not lacking to the individuals. If some spirits declare their incredulity of God's paternal love, it is because they are either incapable or ill due to internal ruins to which they submitted.

Jesus manifests His untiring preoccupation in nurturing the souls of His protégées in a thousand different ways, from the huts of the natives to the cathedrals of the great metropolis.

In those positions of sublime assistance, the individuals learn with their gradual effort, to nourish themselves spiritually, until bringing the church into their home, and transporting it from the domestic sanctuary into their own heart.

Few people meditate over the importance of the infinite mercy of this edificating mass of religious ideas in the world.

The Master is inclined toward the good of all men. Filled with love and abnegation He knows how to nourish with specific resources the ignorant and the wise, the believer and the questioner, the rebel and the unfortunate one. Better than anyone else, Jesus understands that any other way, the individuals would fall exhausted through the immense cliffs that border on the evolutionary path.

# 125

## THE SEPARATION

*"But I tell you the truth: It is for your good that I am
going away." Jesus (John, 16:7)*

Such a statement from Jesus resounds in our innermost
fibers.

No one had a capacity to love greater than Him, yet, He
was the first to recognize the importance of His departure, in
favor of His companions.

What would have happened if Jesus had insisted on
remaining?

Probably the multitudes of Earth would have accentuated
their selfish tendencies, consolidating them.

Because the Divine Friend had searched for Lazarus in the
grave, no one else would be resigned to the separation by death.
Because He had cared for and cleansed some lepers, no one, in

the future, would accept the beneficial cooperation of annoying physical disturbances. The logical result would have been a general interruption in the evolutionary mechanism of Earth.

It was important for the Master to absent Himself, so that the personal effort of each individual could be visible in the Divine Plan of the world's project. Any other way, it would have contributed to the perpetuation of indolence of some and selfishness of others.

Under different aspects the great hour of the evangelical family in our groups with affinity is repeated daily

How often will widowhood, orphanhood, suffering from being apart, perplexity and pain, surge as an elevated convenience for the common good?

Recall the following passage from the Gospel, when separation causes you tears, because if the death of the physical body is a renovation for the departed one, it is also a new life for those who remain.

# 126

## THE THORN

*"To keep me from becoming conceited because of these*
*surpassingly great revelations, there was given*
*me a thorn in my flesh, a messenger of Satan,*
*to torment me." Paul (II Corinthians, 12:7)*

It is extremely dangerous for an individual to be boastful presuming to be unaware of the arduous service in which he is obliged daily to give difficult testimonies. It is a mental situation that is not only menacing but false, because in one unexpected instant, the thorn of the heart will appear.

The prudent disciple shall instill confidence without boasting, thereby revealing himself to be valuable without being ostentatious. He recognizes the extent of his own debts with the Master, but does not feel glorified himself, as he is aware that all the glory belongs to Him, the Master.

There are more than a few men in the world lacking in vigilance and anxiety, who after having received the incense of the multitude move on to harden the bitterness of loneliness; many are content while in the heights of fame, as if they were to remain eternal idols only to cry alone, with the thorn they had ignored, in the depth of their soul.

How can we assume the role of infallible teacher when we are but simple apprentices?

Would it not be more justifiable to serve the Lord, as a youngster or in old age, during abundance or during scarcity, in the administration or as subordinates, with a pondering spirit, observing our vulnerable areas, in the insufficiency and imperfection of what we have been until now?

Let us remember that Paul of Tarsus had been with Jesus personally; he was appointed for divine service in Antioch by the voices from Heaven; fought, worked, and suffered for the Gospel of the Kingdom and in writing to the Corinthians, although quite aged and tired, still referred to the thorn that he was given so that he would not become personally exalted in the sublime tasks of the revelations.

# 127

## THE LAW OF RETURN

*"And come out, those who have done good will rise to live,*
*and those who have done evil will rise to be*
*condemned." Jesus (John, 5:29)*

In rare passages of the Gospel the law of reincarnation appears as clearly as this one here, in the lesson that Jesus presents on the resurrection of the condemnation.

How would the theologians, who are interested in the existence of a burning and eternal Hell, understand these words?

Individuals dedicated to righteousness will find the fountain of life bathing in the waters of corporeal death. Their realizations of the future continue in justifiable ascent directly along with the persevering efforts that they developed on their sanctifying spiritual path. Still, those that are complacent about evil cancel their very own possibility of resurrection in the light.

They are obliged to repeat the expiatory course.

It is the return to the lesson or to the remedy.

No other alternative exists.

The law of the return, then, is clearly contained in that synthesis of Jesus.

Resurrection is reappearance. The understanding of renovation does not correspond to the theory of eternal sorrows.

In the summary and definite sentence there is no recourse to salvation. But by the reference made by Jesus, we observe that Divine Providence is much richer and magnanimous than it appears.

There will be a resurrection for all, except that, those who are righteous, will have it in a new life, and those that are evil, in a new condemnation, as a consequence of their reprehensible behavior.

# 128

## BECAUSE OF IGNORANCE

*"They will do such things because they have not known the Father or me." Jesus (John, 16:3)*

Quite often, painful perplexities face the disciples inspiring them to question.

Why is there disharmony with regards to fraternal efforts?

The journey toward righteousness encounters somber barriers.

The establishment of the light is projected, but the darkness penetrates the path. Simple projects are formulated for charity, which ill intentions attempt to interrupt at the first moment of its realization.

As a rule, the destructive demonstrations originate from distinguished individuals, who due to circumstances act as guides of the general thoughts. They, in the majority of the occasions, are the ones who instigate, through their discourses, impositions and improper demands.

However, the sincere apprentice of Jesus should not waste time with questions and anxieties that are not justified.

The Divine Master clarified this great problem in advance.

Ignorance is the common source of unbalance. If this or that group of individuals tries to impede the manifestation of goodness, it is due to the lack of knowledge, at this time, of the blessings from Heaven.

It is no more than this.

It is essential, therefore, to disregard the darkness that still dominates the greater part of Earth, allowing each apprentice to live in the Light that palpitates in the service to the Lord.

# 129

## WHEN HE BROKE THE BREAD

*"Then the two told them what had happened on the way,
and how Jesus was recognized by them when he
broke the bread." (Luke, 24:35)*

The passage, in which the Master is recognized by His disciples as they desperately marched to Emmaus, is of great importance.

Jesus was following them, as an unseen friend, setting the truth in their hearts with warm, sweet formulas.

During the greater part of the crossing they were in the company of this wise loving man. Both of them considered the stranger to be agreeable and generous. But they only recognized their dear Master when He cut the bread.

The two apprentices had not been able to identify Him, not by His words, nor by His affectionate gestures; but, as soon as the material bread appeared, all their doubts disappeared, and they believed.

Isn't this the same thing that has been occurring in the world for millenniums?

Multitudes of candidates of the faith separate themselves from the divine service, for not having been able to achieve, after certain expectations, the immediate advantages that they had expected in everyday life. Without financial guarantees, without capricious desires satisfied, they do not partake communion in a respectful, faithful and renovating belief.

It is necessary to combat such shortsightedness of the soul.

Blessed be the Lord for the lessons and testimonies, He confers on us; but, you will be very far from the truth if you seek Him solely in the division of the fragmentary and perishable assets.

# 130

## WHERE ARE THEY?

*"Take my yoke upon you and learn from me, for I am
gentle and humble in heart, and you will find rest
for your souls." Jesus (Matthew, 11:29)*

Jesus directed His attention to the multitude of afflicted and
disenchanted, and proclaimed His divine desire to alleviate
them.

"Come to me," exclaimed the Master, "Take my yoke upon
you and learn from me, for I am gentle and humble in heart."

His loving plea vibrated throughout the world and
through all the centuries of Christianity.

Dense is the mob of the desperate and the oppressed of
the Earth; thus, the warm friendly invitation.

It is just that in the words "Come to me" the Master
naturally hopes that those sad anxious souls would seek Him in

order to acquire the Divine teaching. However, not all the afflicted intend to renounce the object of their despair, nor all those with sadness desire to flee from the shadow in order to encounter the light.

The majority of the discouraged try to satisfy their capricious criminal actions with the protection of Jesus, while emitting strange pleas.

However, when the sufferers sincerely direct their thoughts to the Christ, they will hear Him, in the silence of their inner sanctuary, inciting them to despise the reprehensible disputes of the inferior self.

Where are they, the afflicted of Earth who intend to change the captivity of their own passions for the gentle yoke of Jesus Christ?

For them were those saintly words pronounced, "Come to me," reserving for them the powerful light of the Gospel for their indispensable renovation.

# 131

## THE WORLD AND THE FAITH

*"Let this Christ, this King of Israel, come now from
the cross, that we may see and believe."*
(Mark, 15:32)

There are very few men with the capacity for genuine comprehension of the pure belief in their essential value; therefore, we encounter those that slandered the Christ in order to confirm him.

The miracle mentality always swam on the surface of the senses without reaching the zone of the eternal spirit, and if it does not reach the undignified end to which it is aimed, it will result in mordacious challenges.

In the case of the Master, these observations do not stem solely from the populace. Mark asserts that the principal priests also participate in these insulting movements with the scribes, as if to say that the intellect does not translate into a higher spiritual level.

The demonstrators remained deaf toward the Glad Tidings of the Kingdom, blind in noticing the benefits received, and insensitive to the loving touch that Jesus directed to all the hearts.

They intended to have a mere spectacle; expectant that, Christ should descend from the Cross, as if by magic, and all the problems of the inferior faith would be resolved.

The Divine appealer, however, did not give another response other than through silence, in an effort to make them understand the magnitude of His gesture, inaccessible to the childish request of the inquirers.

If you are a sincere student of the Gospel, do not forget that even today, the situation is not too different.

Work ponderously in the service of faith.

Unite with the Lord, give your all you can in His name and proceed in service for the expansion of righteousness, fully convinced that the vast majority of the inferior world will only ask of you, maliciously, distractions and signs.

# 132

## IN EVERYTHING

*"We commend ourselves in every way: in great endurance;
in troubles, hardships and distresses."*
Paul (II Corinthians, 6:4)

The majority of the students of the Gospel do not face the depth of religion seriously in life, but rather, only in the exterior worship. In the conception of many, it will be enough for them to earnestly attend the assemblies of faith, and with that, all the enigmas of the soul in the chapter of our relations with God will be deciphered.

However, the teachings of the Christ appeal towards a renovation and individual improvement in all circumstances.

What can we say of an individual who is apparently contrite in religious activities, confesses publicly in his own faith, but uses profanity in the sanctuary of his home? There are many who declare themselves to be believers in the multitudes, revealing laziness in their work, despair when in pain, insatiable in happiness, unfaithful in the facilities, and blasphemous in the anxieties of the heart.

With what motive would Jesus persist in the formation of His followers, only to have them light incense a few hours per week while kneeling? To attribute such matters to the Master would be to reduce His sublime principles.

It is indispensable that the students improve in every way, demonstrating the excellence of the ideas that nourish them, at home, as well as in the churches, in the private services, as well as in the public areas.

Certainly, no one will be obliged to live exclusively with their hands clasped in adoration, nor their eyes firmly fixed on the Heavens; however, let us not forget that gentleness, good will, cooperation, and fine manners compose a divine part of the living prayer in the apostolate of the Christ.

# 133

## THE GREAT FUTURE

*"But now my kingdom is from another place."*
Jesus (John, 18:36)

From the beginnings of Christianity we have observed students deliberately retiring from the activities of this world, alleging that the Kingdom of the Lord does not belong to Earth.

They kneel for an undetermined time in the establishments of adoration, and actually believe to find, in this flight, the realization of sanctity.

Many cross their arms when facing regenerative services, and when questioned, express resentment for the disagreeable pictures that the terrestrial experience offers them, reporting to the Christ in front of Pilate, when the Master assured that His Kingdom was not, as yet, installed in the circles of human struggle.

However, it is justifiable to consider that the Christ did not disinherit the planet. His word did not support an absolute denial of Celestial happiness for the Earth, but rather, solely defined the existent landscape at that time, not forgetting about the hope in the future.

The Master, clarified: "but for now my Kingdom is not of this world."

This affirmative response reveals His confidence.

Jesus, therefore, cannot endorse the false notion of the discouraged workers, simply because the shadow became denser due to transitory problems, or because human wounds become more painful. Such occurrences are sometimes the result of pure visual illusion.

Divine activity never ceases and, particularly, in the area of beneficial struggle where the student will carve his own victory.

It is not logical, therefore, to desert merely for an attitude of contemplation, but rather, to advance confidently toward a great future.

# 134

## SPIRITUAL NUTRITION

*"It is good for our hearts to be strengthened by grace, not
by ceremonial foods, which are of no value to those
who eat them." Paul (Hebrews, 13:9)*

There are nutritional vices of the soul, just as there are
nutritional vices of the body.

Many persons substitute pure water for inciting drinks, as
occurs to many people who prefer to deal with a pernicious
illusion regarding spiritual problems.

The nourishment of the heart, in order to be effective in
the eternal life, shall be based on the simple realities of the
evolutionary road.

It is crucial that we be fortified with illuminative values,
without paying attention to the dazzling fantasies that come
from the exterior. It is precisely on a religious path that such care
and efforts demand a greater amount of evolvement.

The believer, as a rule, is always thirsting for situations that can satisfy his toxic whims, like a gourmet desires exotic dishes. However, in the same manner as these pleasures of the table in no way benefits the individuals' essential activities, the sensations learned in the zone of phenomena become useless to the spirit when it does not possess the sufficient interior resources to comprehend the ultimate purpose. Numerous apprentices regard their respective religious experience, as a purely intellectual matter. But, it is indispensable to recognize that the nourishment of the soul, in order to become molded, definitely, requires a sincere heart interested in the divine truths. When an individual places himself in this intimate position, he truly becomes fortified for the sublimation, because he recognizes so much material of dignified labor around his steps, that any transitory sensation to him, becomes localized at the last stepping stones on the path.

# 135

## NECESSARY RENOVATION

*"Do not put out the Spirit's fire."*
*Paul (I Thessalonians, 5:19)*

When the Apostle of the gentiles wrote this exhortation, he did not intend it to mean that the spirit, could be destroyed, but rather, he intended to renovate the mental attitude of so many who live actively suffocating their superior spiritual tendencies.

It is not rare to observe individuals acting against their own conscience in order to avoid being categorized as spiritual. In spite of this, the incarnate entities remain within the laborious apprenticeship in order to lift themselves from the world as glorious spirits. This is the greatest goal of the human schooling.

However, individuals linger at a distance from the great truth. They habitually prefer the rigorous conventionalism, and only in a costly way open their understanding to the realities of the soul. Customs are evidently a strong and determining element in the evolution; however, only when they are inspired by principles of a superior order.

It is necessary, therefore, not to asphyxiate the seeds of an edificating life that are born daily in the hearts influenced by our Merciful Father.

We have some companions that return from Earth through the same door of ignorance and indifference through which they had entered. This is the reason why as the disciples balance their daily activities they should ask themselves: What did I accomplish today? Did I accentuate the strokes of the inferior individual of yesterday or did I develop the elevated qualities of the spirit that I wish to retain for tomorrow?

# 136

## CONFLICT

*"So I find this law at work: When I want to do good,*
*evil is right there with me."*
*Paul (Romans, 7:21)*

The sincere disciples of the Gospel, as described by Paul of
Tarsus, encounter enormous conflicts in their own being.

As a rule, they confront enormous difficulties in their
testimonies. In the precise instance that they wish to reveal the
presence of the Divine Companion in their heart, one word and
one momentary attitude betrays them before their very
conscience, indicating the persistence of prior weaknesses.

The majority experience sensations of shame and pain.

Some attribute those falls to the influence of evil spirits,
and generally seek this enemy in an exterior plane, when in
actuality they should heal the undesirable cause within, which
places them in tune with evil vibrations.

It is unquestionable that we still find ourselves very far from a region in which we can be exempt from adverse vibrations; however, it is important to verify the observation given by Paul within each one of us.

While mankind maintains itself either in cold indifference or in restless obstinacy, it is not called upon to a pure analysis; however, as soon as it awakens to the renovation, its inner camp turns into a battlefield.

Against this oscillating aspiration for righteousness, each day that goes by, a heavy baggage of accumulated shadows rises in our soul that has transpired in prior centuries. It is indispensable, therefore, that we observe great serenity and resistance on our part in order that the progress, thus achieved, is not lost.

The Lord concedes us the clarity of today so that we might forget the darkness of yesterday in preparation for tomorrow, on the path of the imperishable light.

# 137

## ENEMIES

*"But love your enemies."*
*Jesus (Luke, 6:35)*

This affirmation made by the Divine Master, merits meditation everywhere. Logically, this recommendation referring to "love your enemies" requires a special analysis.

The multitude, generally speaking, attributes the verb "to love" to activities involving caresses. In order for an individual to demonstrate affection before common eyes, he would have to use voluminous words and tender demonstrations, when we know that love can actually shine in the hearts of any being without any superficial demonstration. Because the Father confers us difficult and rugged experiences on Earth or in other worlds, we cannot attribute to Him any denial of His love.

In the area that the Divine Friend is alluding to, we are justified in giving it our legitimate consideration.

Where there is strife there is antagonism, revealing the prior existence of circumstances with which it would not be fair to agree, as it involves the common good. When the Master suggested that we love our enemies, He did not insist on our applauding the one who deliberately steals or destroys, nor did He request that we multiply the wings of perversity or ill-intention. He recommended actually that we aid the cruelest; however, not by incorrectly bestowing our approval, but rather, by demonstrating a genuine fraternal desire to instill in him to follow a divine path, through patience, through reconstructive resources or through a restoring labor. The Master, above all, was preoccupied in preserving us from the poison of hate, avoiding our great fall into inferior uselessness and destructive disputes.

Therefore, love those that appear to be in opposition to your heart, supporting them fraternally with all the possibilities of assistance at your reach, fully convinced that such a measure will free you of the calamitous duel of evil against evil.

# 138

## LET US ANALYZE THIS

*"For Christ did not send me to baptize, but to preach the*
*Gospel – not with words of human wisdom, lest the*
*cross of Christ be emptied of its power."*
*Paul (I Corinthians, 1:17)*

Generally speaking, while we are incarnates, we take great pride in attracting as many people as possible to our way of thinking.

Invariably we are good speakers and eminently subtle in presenting reasoning that overwhelms the point of view of those that cannot comprehend us in the immediacy of the struggle.

On our first small triumph, we become wearisome researching holy books, not in order to acquire a more vast illumination, but rather, with the objective of investigating the writings of the Divine Scriptures, seeking to accentuate the vulnerable affirmations of our opponents.

If we are Roman Catholics, we insist that our friends go to mass and take the sacraments; if we are adepts of the reformed churches, we insist on their appearance at the external worship; and if we are spiritists, we seek to multiply the number of spiritist sessions we have with the invisible plane.

This effort is not less commendable in some of its characteristics; however, it is imperative to remember that the student of the Gospel, who sincerely tries to understand the Christ, feels invigorated in his intimate conduct.

When Jesus penetrates the heart of an individual, He converts him into a living testimony of righteousness, and directs him to evangelize his brothers, with his own life. When an individual finds Jesus, he does not stop short, purely and simply pronouncing brilliant words; rather, he lives in accordance with the Master, exemplifying the work and the love that illuminate life, so that the glory of the cross shall not be in vain.

# 139

## Offerings

*"He sacrificed for their sins once for all when he offered
himself." Paul (Hebrews, 7:27)*

Human beings, as a rule, feel rather comfortable in an
opulent home, under a sky of blue.

Meanwhile, when the difficulties surge they immediately
seek out someone to substitute them in places of boredom and
pain. They often pay a heavy price for this escape, and
indefinitely postpone the beneficial experience to which they
were invited by the hand of the Lord.

It is because of this that the religious leaders of all times,
establish complicated problems with the offerings bestowed by
the faithful.

In the primitive rituals there was no hesitation in
sacrificing the young and the children.

In the course of time man reverted to sacrificing sheep, bulls, and goats in the sanctuaries.

For centuries the habit of offering coins, precious objects, and riches endured, which were delegated for service of the worship.

But, with all these demonstrations, the human being seeks only to incur individual favoritism from God, as if the Father were so inclined with earthly matters.

The majority of those that make material offerings, do not act in this manner in the places of worship due to their love of the divine work; but rather, with the deliberate purpose of buying favors from Heaven, excluding themselves from their personal inner edification.

However, in this sense the Christ provided a most precious response to the students of the world. Far from arguing over any prerogatives, He did not send any substitutes to the Calvary, nor animals to be sacrificed in the temples; but rather, He personally embraced the heavy wooden cross, sacrificing Himself in favor of all human beings, thereby demonstrating that each of His followers shall be compelled to offer his own personal testimony at the altar of his own personal life.

# 140

## LET US REMEMBER CORRECTLY

*"Remember my chains."*
Paul (Colossians, 4:18)

In the customary childish reflections, the believers only remember the luminous aura of the spirits formerly sanctified on Earth.

Many imagine they will find them easily far away from beyond the grave, in order to receive precious remembrances from them.

They consider the Heavens as a brilliant resting place in the immensity of the cosmos.

How many will only remember Paul at his glorification? Meanwhile, in this observation to the Colossians, the great Apostle exhorts his friends to remember the prisons, as if to say, that the disciples should not maintain their thoughts in the foresight of celestial facilities, but rather, seriously reflect upon the proper work required to achieve the Divine Kingdom.

The conquest of sublime spirituality also has its avenues. It is indispensable to travel through them.

Before fixing our sight on the brilliant crown of the faithful Apostles, let us meditate on the thorns that wounded their forehead.

Paul was able to achieve these culminations, but how many assaults from the whips, racks and irony did he have to bear while adapting to the teachings of the Christ, as he scaled the mountains!

Do not notice solely the superiority manifested in those to whom you consecrate admiration and respect. Do not forget to imitate them adapting yourself to the sacrificing services to which they devoted themselves in order to reach the divine end.

# 141

## FRATERNAL LOVE

*"Keep on loving each other as brothers."*
*Paul (Hebrews, 13:1)*

The family affections, the family ties, the natural attractions, can be manifestations of a pure soul when the individual elevates them to the altar of a superior sentiment; nevertheless, it is reasonable for the spirit not to fall from the weight of his personal inclinations.

Equilibrium is the ideal position.

Because of excessive protection, innumerable parents cause their children harm.

Owing to excessive preoccupations, many married couples descend to the caverns of despair, being confronted by the insatiable monsters of jealousy, which annihilates their happiness.

Due to lack of vigilance, beautiful friendships terminate in the abyss of the shadows.

The evangelic call, for this reason, is of great importance.

Pure fraternity is the most sublime system of relationships between souls.

The individual, who feels that he is a child of God and a sincere brother to others, is not a victim of the phantoms of grudge, envy, ambition or mistrust. Those who love one another fraternally, are happy with the joy of their companions, and feel pleased with the good fortune that visits their fellow man.

The violent friendships commonly known on Earth, pass by volcanically and uselessly.

In the web of the successive reincarnations, the affective titles go through constant modifications. It is so because the fraternal love, sublime and pure, representing the supreme objective of the efforts toward understanding, is the imperishable light that will survive in the eternal journey.

# 142

# REPRISALS

*"The very fact that you have lawsuits among you means
you have been completely defeated already. Why not
rather be wronged? Why not rather be cheated?"*
Paul (I Corinthians, 6:7)

Demands do not always remain in the Courts of Justice, in the shocking field of public processes.

They are expressed on a greater scale in the homes and in the institutions. There, they are activated through the mental disorders and through scandalous conversation, in the invisible mud of hatred, which asphyxiates the hearts and annuls energy. Overall, if they do exist, it is due to the components of the family or of the associations that feed them with the oil of continued animosity.

Numerous apprentices become victims of similar disturbances due to their retention of false regenerating principals.

In general, a great number prefer to use a more aggressive attitude, with sword in hand, wielding it supposedly to secure the improvement of others.

Ready to protest, to accuse, to criticize loudly, usually declaring that they represent the truth. But why not exemplify their own personal faith, by withstanding the injustice and pain heroically, in the silence of a faithful soul, prior to the option of any reply?

How many homes would be happier, how many institutions would be converted into permanent springs of light, if the believers of the Gospel would learn to remain silent, thus speaking at the propitious time, advantageously?

This reference made is not directed to vulgar men, but rather, to the disciples of Jesus.

What a great advantage the world would gain, when the follower of the Christ can feel happiness in being a simple instrument of righteousness in the Divine Hands, forgetting the old objective of being the arbitrary instructor of Celestial Service?

# 143

## DO NOT TYRANNIZE

*"With many similar parables Jesus spoke the word
to them, as much as they could understand."*
(Mark, 4:33)

In the dissemination of the Evangelical teachings, every now and then, we encounter preachers who are strict and demanding.

Such an anomaly is not only seen in the general service. In the personal sphere it is not uncommon to see severe and fervent friends, who desperately demand that the followers be in tune with the religious principles that they embrace.

Harsh discussions arise touching off poisonous bitterness.

Beautiful afective expressions are shaken in their foundation, due to improper offenses.

However, if the disciple is truly controlled by his determination to be united with the Master, such an attitude can be easily corrected.

The Master would only speak to those who listened "as much as they could understand."

To the Apostles, He conferred instructions of an elevated symbolic value, while to the multitude He transmitted fundamental truths by way of simple stories. His speech varied according to the spiritual needs of those who gathered around Him. He absolutely never violated anyone's personal position.

If you are in service to the Lord, consider the indispensable requirements of illumination, as the world is in dire need of Christian workers, and not of doctrinaire tyrants.

# 144

## MAKE PREPARATIONS

*"He will show you a large upper room, all furnished.*
*Make preparations there."*
Jesus (Luke, 22:12)

That furnished "upper room" to which Jesus referred is a perfect symbol of the internal lodging of the soul.

Viewing Nature, which offers such wonderful lessons in all areas of activity, we observe that men await each day always renewing the dispositions of the home. Here, we sweep the waste, there walls are ornamented. The furniture, usually the same ones, are put through a daily cleaning process.

The conscientious individual will recognize that the majority of his actions in the physical experience are involved in incessant preparation for the life that he will face beyond the death of the body.

If this occurs in the physical existence on Earth, what can we not say about the appropriate spiritual effort for the eternal path?

Without a doubt, numerous people will go through each day in an irrational manner, moving about mechanically. They arise from bed, feed the perishable body, are absorbed with trifles, then return to sleep again, each night.

The sincere apprentice does know that he has reached the symbolic "upper room" of his heart. Although he is not able to change his ideas daily, as occurs with the furniture in the residence, he gives them a new shine frequently, by improving the impulses, renovating conceptions, elevating wishes, and always improving the laudable qualities that he already possesses.

The individual that is simply a materialist awaits the future of a physical organic death; the spiritual individual awaits the Divine Master, in order to consolidate his personal redemption.

Do not abandon, therefore, the "upper room" of faith, and there in make preparations for constant ascension.

# 145

## WORKERS

*"Do your best to present yourself to God as one approved, a
workman who does not need to be ashamed."*
Paul (II Timothy, 2:15)

Since time immemorial, individuals have been idealizing a
thousand ways in which to present themselves before God
and His messengers.

Many people worry throughout an entire existence on how
to ready their clothes for the celestial concert, while numerous
believers take careful notes about the bitter trials on Earth, for
the purpose of unthreading an immense rosary of complaints
before the Father, in order to stand out in the future world.

The majority of devotees desire to initiate the trip, beyond
the death, with saintly titles; however, there is no realistic way to
reflect our true position than the one we find ourselves in, as
workers.

The world is a department of the Divine Home.

Professorships and the hoe do not constitute elements of embarrassing divisions, but rather, hierarchical steps for different cooperators.

The edifying path unfolds for everyone.

Here caves are opened up in the productive soil, over there they browse through books for the road of the intelligence, but the spirit is the living foundation of the manifested service.

The workers are classified in different positions, but the field is only one.

Realistically speaking, then, let no one be concerned with titles and awards, because the work is complex in all the sectors of dignifying activity and the result is always the fruit of a well lived cooperation. This is the reason why we conclude with Paul that the greatest victory of the disciple will be on the day that he presents himself to the Lord as an approved worker.

# 146

# FOLLOW THE TRUTH

*"Instead, speaking the truth in love, we will in all things
grow up into him who is the Head, that is, Christ."*
Paul (Ephesians, 4:15)

Because truth is relative, numerous thinkers take the road of absolute negativism, converting materialism into a zone of extreme intellectual disorder.

How can we interpret the truth if it appears to be so obscure to the ordinary methods of appreciation?

Boasting over superiority, the officious scientist assures that what is real does not go beyond the organized forms, just as the fanatic, who admits the divine revelation only in the circle of dogmas that he embraces.

Paul, however, offers a rewarding indication to those who wish to penetrate the dominion of the highest knowledge.

It is essential to follow the truth in charity, without intending to incarcerate it in the prison of restricted definition.

Let us convert into love the noble teachings we have received. Truth summed up with charity presents spiritual progress as a result of the effort. Without taking care of this prerequisite, we will be surprised by vigorous obstacles on the path of sublimation. We are required to grow in every way that experience offers us of usefulness and beauty for the eternity with Jesus Christ; however, we will not achieve its realization, without transforming, daily, the small parcel of truth that we possess into love for our fellow man.

Comprehension seeks reality, in the same manner as reality seeks comprehension.

Therefore, let us be genuine, but above all, let us be righteous.

# 147

# IT IS NOT SOLELY THAT

*"But now you must rid yourselves of all such things as*
*these: anger, rage, malice, slander, and filthy*
*language from your lips."*
Paul (Colossians, 3:8)

In religious activity, many individuals believe that the reform of the personality begins from the moment that the disciple of the faith disassociates himself from certain material wealth.

An individual that distributes a large amount of clothes and food among the needy is recognized as being renewed in the Lord; although, this constitutes a form of true transformation, it does not represent the entirety of all the corresponding characteristics.

Some individuals dispose of their wealth in favor of charity, but they do not cede in their personal opinion, in the sublime effort of renunciation.

Enormous rows of apprentices proclaim to be in readiness for the practice of goodness; however, they insist that charitable services be executed according to their whims, but not according to Jesus.

All over, one can hear fervent promises of fidelity to Christ; however, no one will achieve this realization without observing the conjunction of necessary obligations.

A minor miscalculation in its construction can betray the equilibrium of an entire building. That is why when one dispossesses himself of any material patrimony, in favor of others, let him not forget to disintegrate in his very own steps, the old package of grudges, of the capricious illnesses, of quick judgments, or of criminal frailties, within which we maintain a masked face in order to appear that, which we are not.

# 148

## HARVESTERS

> *"Then he said to his disciples: The harvest is plentiful
> but the workers are few"*
> *(Matthew, 9:37)*

The lesson here does not refer to the spiritual crop of the great periods of renovation throughout time; but rather, to the harvest of consolations that the Gospel enfolds within it.

On that occasion, mobs of disenchanted and roving hearts remained around the Master, according to the narrative by Matthew, resembling a flock without the shepherd. There were melancholy faces and supplicant eyes in sad disenchantment.

It was then that Jesus erected the symbol of a really great harvest, accompanied by few harvesters.

The Gospel remains in the world as a blessed celestial harvest, destined to enrich the human spirit; meanwhile, the percentage of individuals ready to work in the harvesting is very small. The majority awaits the beneficial wheat or the finished bread for their own nourishment. Rare are those that confront the storms, the rigors of the work and the dangerous surprises that the effort of reaping requires of a devoted and faithful worker.

Because of that, the multitude of the desperate and disillusioned occurs continuously in the world, in increasing rows, throughout the centuries.

The self-sacrificing workers of the Christ proceed charged in virtue of the many hungry that roam around the harvest, lacking the precise courage of personally finding the nourishment of the eternal life. That picture will continue to persist on Earth, until the good consumers also learn to be good harvesters.

# 149

## To believe in vain

*"By this Gospel you are saved, if you hold firmly
to the word I preached to you. Otherwise
you have believed me in vain."*
*Paul (I Corinthians, 15:2)*

As is the case with many flowers that do not reach full bloom in the appropriate season, innumerable souls exist in the service of faith who do not accomplish during long periods of terrestrial struggles their own inner illumination, due to having believed in the paths of life in vain.

Paul of Tarsus was very explicit when he assured the Corinthians that they would be saved if they held on to the Gospel.

The revelation of Jesus is an extensive field in which there is room for all men, referring to the various services.

Many arrive at the work site; however, they do not go beyond the word, cooperating in purely intellectual organizations. Some improvise theological systems, others contribute in statistics, and others are still preoccupied with the historic locality of the Lord.

It is imperative to recognize that any dignified task is useful at its proper time, according to the sentiments of the collaborator; however, regarding the eternal life that Christianity unfolds at a glance, we must retain within us the teaching of the Master looking toward the necessary application.

Each student should be a living page in the book that Jesus is writing with the evolving material of Earth. The disciple should engrave the Gospel in his own existence, or he will have to prepare to restart the apprenticeship once again; because without first fixating within him the light of the lesson, he will have believed in vain.

# 150

## HE IS ONE AND THE SAME

*"The Father Himself loves you."*
*Jesus (John, 16:27)*

Let no one fail to appreciate the values of confidence.

Let no servant flee from the benefit of being cooperative.

He, who today can give away something useful, will possibly require essential cooperation tomorrow.

However, though someone become enriched with fraternity and faith, let him not forget the necessity of the infinite evolvement in righteousness.

The earnest worker of the Gospel should try to avoid pernicious favoritism.

The divine work does not possess privileged ones. In its numerous areas there are more devoted and more faithful workers; nevertheless, they should not be classified as fetishes, but rather, respected and imitated as symbols of loyalty and service.

Creating idols of human beings is worse than raising statues for adoration. The marble is impassive, but the companion is our fellow human being that should never be abused.

Let each individual pay the tribute of his personal effort to life.

The Supreme Father expects only this of us, in order to convert us into direct collaborators.

The Christ Himself affirmed that the Father, who holds Him in high regard, loves all of humanity equally.

The God that inspires the doctor is one and the same as He who protects the sick.

It matters little if Asians and Europeans call Him by different names.

Invariably, He is the same Father.

Let us then, preserve the light of consolation, the blessing of the fraternal assistance, the confidence in our Superior Spiritual Brothers and the certainty of their protection. Above all, let us not forget our natural obligation to follow towards the Heights, making use of our own feet.

# 151

## No One Leaves

> *"Simon Peter answered him. Lord, to whom shall we go?*
> *You have the words of eternal life." (John, 6:68)*

As the Master revealed new characteristics of His doctrine of love, His followers, who were then numerous, were penetrating a vast circle in the domains of responsibilities. Many of them, fearing the obligations that they felt corresponded to them, left discreetly from the sheltering assembly of Capernaum.

The Christ, meanwhile, conscious of the obligation of a divine order, far from violating the principles of liberty, reunited the small assembly that remained, and questioned the disciples:

"You do not want to leave too, do you?"

It was at this time that Peter emitted the wise response engraved forever in the Christian edifice.

Actually, whoever commences the spiritualization service with Jesus, will never again feel identical emotions afar from Him. The sublime experience may at times, be interrupted, but never annihilated. Being obliged on various occasions by impositions from the physical zone, the companion of the Gospel will undergo spiritual accidents, causing a slight halt, however, he will definitely not lose his way.

Whoever takes communion effectively in the banquet of Christian revelation, will not forget the loving Master who addressed the invitation.

For this reason Simon Peter asked accurately:

"Lord, to whom shall we go?"

The world is replete with philosophers, scientists, and reformers of all kinds, without a doubt respected in the advanced human concepts which they proclaim; however, in the majority of situations, they are no more than simple narrators of transitory words, reflecting on ephemeral experiences. Jesus Christ, however, is the Savior of the souls and the Master of the hearts, and with Him we will encounter the routes of the eternal life.

# 152

# IN WHAT MANNER?

*"What do you prefer? Shall I come to you with a whip,*
*or in love and with a gentle spirit."*
Paul (I Corinthians, 4:21)

Sometimes the Apostle of the Gentiles, full of sublime inspirations, presented to his companions interrogating questions, almost cruel if solely considered in the literal sense, but carrying admirable reality when seen through the immortal light.

In all the Christian homes, vibrations of love and peace radiate. Jesus never left His followers forgotten though they were far apart from the path of the interpretations.

Self-sacrificing emissaries of celestial devotion spread sanctifying assistance throughout all the epochs of mankind. History demonstrates this as an irrefutable fact.

No century has ever lacked legitimate missionaries of righteousness.

Promises and revelations from the Lord reach many ports of knowledge in a thousand ways.

The apprentices that join the evangelical ranks, therefore, cannot allege ignorance of the objectives in order to hide their personal failings. Each one, in his own place has received the program of service that he is obliged to execute daily. If they flee from their task and escape the testimony, they will owe said anomaly to their own inactive will.

Because of this, it is possible that the moment will arise in which the lazy pleading disciple will be able to hear the Master without the use of intermediaries, exclaiming in a similar manner:

"What do you prefer? Shall I come to you with a whip, or in love and with a gentle spirit."

# 153

## LET US NOT STUMBLE

*"Jesus answered: Are there not twelve hours of daylight?*
*A man who walks by day will not stumble, for he*
*sees by this world's light." (John, 11:9)*

The context of this question from the Master has a vast significance for the disciples of today.

"Are there not twelve hours of daylight?"

Each one should conscientiously ask themselves in what tasks they are applying such a great patrimony of time.

It is said emphatically that there is a great problem of unemployment in modern days. Nonetheless, whatever crisis of this nature arises will not result from lack of employment, but rather, from the absence of individual good will.

A careful investigation into this matter would reveal the truth. Many individuals remain inactive because they rebel against the type of service that is offered to them, or in nonconformity due to the particular salaries.

Imbalance, immediately takes over.

The laziness of the workers provokes vigilance on the part of the administrators and the laws in the world reflect this animosity and distrust.

If the arms become stationary the factories sleep.

The same thing occurs in the sphere of spiritual action.

How many apprentices abandon their tasks alleging lack of time? How many transfer into zones of laziness, because this or that minor incident occurred, which is in full disagreement with the superior principles that they embrace?

And for nonsense, a great number of vigorous workers seek the rearguard full of shadows. However, those that possess acute hearing can still listen to those words of the Lord: "Are there not twelve hours of daylight? A man who walks by day will not stumble."

# 154

# THE OPPOSERS

*"What, then, shall we say in response to this? If God is*
*for us, who can be against us?"*
Paul (Romans, 8:31)

This question from Paul still represents a beautiful theme for the Evangelical Community of today.

Because of our efforts an immense field unfolds, in which the Master awaits our resolute collaboration.

However, quite often a great number of companions prefer to abandon the construction in order to argue with evildoers on the path.

Adverse elements surround us everywhere.

Unexpected obstacles arise before our grieving eyes; old friends leave us alone; yesterday's favorable conditions become transformed into cruel hostility today.

Enormous rows of workers flee from the danger fearing the storm and forgetting the testimony.

However, we were not situated in this task to surrender to the panic; nor did the Master send us to work with the objective of confusing us through the experiences of the exterior circles.

We were called upon to construct.

Naturally, we must automatically count on the thousand daily eventualities, very probably being born of negative forces, making the construction difficult. Our day of struggle shall be besieged by the disturbances and by the fatigue. This is inevitable in a world that expects everything from the genuine Christian.

Because of this imperative reason between threats and incomprehension on the path, it is logical to inquire, in good humor, as spoken by the Apostle of the gentiles:

"If God is for us, who can be against us?"

# 155

## AGAINST FOOLISHNESS

*"Are you so foolish? After beginning with the spirit, are*
*you now trying to attain your goal by human effort?"*
*Paul (Galatians, 3:3)*

One of the greatest disasters on the path of the disciples is the false comprehension with which they initiate their efforts in the superior regions, marching inversely toward the areas of inferiority. They appear to be similar to the men seeking to find gold and readily accepting the mud of the puddles.

Similar failures are common in the distinct sectors of religious thinking.

We observe the sickly that direct their thoughts to a high spiritual level, absorbing noble impulses, and charged with precious intention; once they are cured, they reflect about the best way to apply the advantages herein obtained toward the acquisition of easy money.

Some, after being assisted by friends from more sublime spheres in transcendental questions of eternal life, wish to attribute to these same benefactors the function of human policemen in their search of undignified objectives.

Numerous students do persist in the work for righteousness; however, when unfavorable moments appear, they submit to discouragement reclaiming a prize for the diminishing years on Earth that they tried to serve in the work of the Divine Master, and completely overlook the multi millenniums, in which the Father has served us.

Such spiritual anomalies that considerably perturb the effort of the disciples, originate from the poisonous filters composed by the great desire for compensation.

Let us strive, then, against the expectation of retribution, so that we can continue in the task commenced in the company of humility, bearer of the imperishable light.

# 156

# HEAVEN UPON HEAVEN

*"But store up for yourselves treasures in heaven, where*
*moth and rust do not destroy, and where*
*thieves do not break in and steal."*
Jesus (Matthew, 6:20)

In all the rows of Christians we encounter some that are ambitious for compensation and presume to observe in the above declaration of Jesus, a positive resource for vengeance against those that, because of their work and devotion, received greater possibilities on Earth.

What appears to be confidence in God is a disguised hatred for their fellow men.

Since they are not able to hoard the financial resources before their eyes, they thrust forth critical and rebellious thoughts waiting for the paradise for their desired revenge.

But, it will not be through the surrendering of the body to the laboratory of Nature that the human personality will automatically find the plans of Glittering Beauty.

Definitely, imperishable sanctuaries shine in the sublime spheres, but it is imperative to consider that, in the immediate regions of human activity, we still find immense copies of moth and thieves, in the evolving rows that extend beyond the grave.

When the Master recommended that we store treasures in Heaven, He was suggesting that we expand the values of righteousness in the peace of the heart. The individual that acquires faith and knowledge, virtue and illumination in the divine innermost recesses of the conscience, is in possession of the celestial path. He, who applies the redeeming principles that he embraces, finishes by conquering that precious card; and he who works daily in the practice of righteousness, automatically lives accumulating riches in the Peaks of Life.

Let no one be fooled in this sense.

Far, far away from Earth, the Lord radiates His blessings from the Celestial Heights; however, it is necessary to possess light in order to perceive them.

It is the Law that the Divine Will be identified with that which is Divine; but no one will be able to contemplate the Heavens if they shelter a hell in their heart.

# 157

## THE SELFISH SON

*"But he answered his father. Look, all these years
I've been slaving for you and never disobeyed
your orders. Yet you never gave me even a
young goat so I could celebrate with my
friends." (Luke, 15:32)*

This parable does not only introduce the prodigal son; with a sharper attention we will also encounter the selfish son.

This veiled teaching from the Master demonstrates the two extremes of filial ingratitude. One stays in squandering, the other in avarice. These are the two extremes that enfold the circle of human incomprehension.

Generally speaking, believers only distinguish the son that abandoned the paternal home in order to live in extravagant scandal, turning into the creditor of all the punishments; and few students were able to fix their thoughts on the condemnable conduct of the brother who remained under the family roof, not any less subjected to reprehension.

Observing the paternal generosity, the inferior sentiments that influence him rise to the surface in demonstrations of selfishness.

The vibrations of love that reign in the homes' domestic ambient bother him. He alleges, as does a lazy person, his years of service in the family and invokes, as would a vain believer, the supposed observance of the Divine Law, thus disrespecting the father, incapable of sharing his just contentment.

This type of selfish individual is considered vulgar in everyday life. Before considering the well being and happiness of the others, he rebels and suffers through the indifference that is killing him, and the envy that is poisoning him.

When we read this parable attentively, we ignore which of the sons is the most unfortunate, if it is the prodigal one or the selfish one; but we dare to believe in the immense unhappiness of the second one, as the first already possessed the blessing of remorse in his favor.

# 158

# THE INTERNAL GOVERNMENT

*"I beat my body and make it my slave so that after
I have preached to others, I myself will not be
disqualified for the prize."*
Paul (I Corinthians, 9:27)

In effect, the body is a miniature of the Universe.

It is indispensable, therefore, that we learn how to govern it.

As an earthly material representation of the spiritual personality, it is reasonable that each one of us be attentive to its needs. It is not that passive substance has acquired more power than the human will; however, it is imperative to recognize that the inferior tendencies are intent on extracting from us the power of control.

It is important that each individual be alert as to his or her own government.

The internal life, in some ways, resembles the life of a State. The spirit assumes the control assisted by various ministries, such as that of reflection, knowledge, understanding, respect and orderliness. Diverse and simultaneous thoughts represent good or bad pleas from the inner parliament. In the depth of each mind, extensive potential for progress and sublimation exists, claiming work.

The supreme governor which is the spirit, in the cellular cosmos, issues beneficial laws, but does not always mobilize the inspecting organs of individual will. The inferior zones then continue in their prior disorders, not caring about the renovating decrees that they neither defy nor execute. When this anomaly occurs the individual goes on to become a living enigma, when not converted into a blind or perverse person.

Whoever expects a healthy life, without self-discipline is not far from a ruinous or total imbalance.

It is necessary to install our individual personal government into every position in life. The fundamental problem is to observe a strong will toward ourselves and goodwill toward our fellow man.

# 159

## THE POSSESION OF THE KINGDOM

*"Strengthening the disciples and encouraging them*
*to remain true to the faith. We must go through*
*many hardships to enter the Kingdom*
*of God." (Acts, 14:22)*

The Gospel fools no one in its teachings.

The preoccupations of the believers intending to suborn the Divine forces is vulgar. But, it will not be at the price of many masses, many hymns, and numerous psychic spiritual sessions, that the individual will effect the sublime acquisition of lofty spirituality.

Naturally, all edificating practice must be taken advantage of as a helpful element; however, every human being is compelled in his personal efforts toward illumination.

The Glad Tidings do not distribute indulgences at the world's price, and each person encounters innumerable paths toward ascension.

Temples and instructors multiply and each one offers parcels of help or assistance, in the orientation service. However, the entrance and possession of eternal inheritance is verified by way of just .

This is not accidental. It is a necessary and logical measure.

No rare statues are improvised without the action of the chisel, just as the wheat is not picked unless the soil has been tilled.

More than a few apprentices are accustomed to interpreting certain advice from the Gospel as excessive exhortation to suffering; however, what appears to them to be an obsession for pain, is imperative for the education of the soul for eternal life.

There will not be one individual able to find infinite estuary of the divine energy without undergoing the tribulations of Earth.

Personality without a struggle, on the Planetary Crust, is a narrow soul. Only work and self-sacrifice, difficulties and obstacles, as elements for progress and personal improvement can give the individual truthful assessment of his grandeur.

# 160

## THE GREAT STRUGGLE

> *"For we do not wrestle against flesh and blood, but*
> *against principalities, against powers, against*
> *the rulers of the darkness of this age, against*
> *spiritual hosts of wickedness in the heavenly*
> *places." Paul (Ephesians, 6:12)*

According to our reiterated affirmations, the great struggle does not actually reside in the blood and flesh, but rather, with our inferior spiritual dispositions.

Paul of Tarsus acted superbly inspired, when he wrote his recommendation to his companions of Ephesus.

The silent and incessant conflict between the earnest disciples and the forces of the shadows is found in our own personal nature, because we became open accomplices with evil in our not remote past.

We have been declared participants in unlawful actions in celestial places.

And even today, between the condensed fluids of the flesh or in the closer spheres, we act in the service of self-restoration in plain paradise.

The Earth is also a sublime stepping stone toward Heaven.

When someone refers to the fallen angels, the human listeners immediately get an impression of a superb and mysterious palace from which wise and luminous beings are expelled.

Isn't it also similar to the educated individual who turns into an assassin in front of a university or a temple?

Generally, the observer on Earth relates to the crime; however, he does not stop to analyze the sacred and respectable place in which it occurred.

The great struggle that the Apostle refers to continues incessantly.

The cities and the human constructions are celestial zones. Neither they, nor the organic cells that are of service to us, constitute the powerful enemies, but rather, "the spiritual forces of evil," with which we synchronize through the inferior areas that we desperately hold on to. They are a vast group of souls and somber thoughts that obscure human vision, and operate cunningly so as not to lose their active companions of yesterday.

# 161

## WHAT DO YOU SAY?

*"But what about you? He asked. Who do you think I am?"*
*(Luke, 9:20)*

In worldly discussions, there shall always be writers and scientists ready to examine the Master, in their pattern of pure intellectual impressions under the itching of human presumption.

But those friends did not have contact with the soul of the Gospel. They did not go beyond the academic circles, nor did they risk conventional titles in a dispassionate excursion through the divine revelation; therefore, they will naturally continue to be fooled by their vanity, by their prejudice or by the fear that are typical to their transitory manner of being, until they are moved by the personal experiences encountered on the paths of eternal life.

Meanwhile, in the intimacy of the sincere and faithful apprentices, the question asked by Jesus takes on singular importance.

Each one of us should have our own personal opinion, relative to the wisdom and to the mercy with which we have been blessed.

Vain conversations regarding the Christ fit in, solely, with those disoriented spirits on the road of life. But we are obliged to give testimony regarding our intimate relationship with the Lord, as we are direct possessors of His infinite mercy. Let us meditate and renew our aspirations in His Gospel of Love, recognizing perfectly well the inappropriate mutual appeals made with regards to the Master. The sublime question comes to each one of us from Him, and we should all know Him in order to incorporate Him in our daily tasks.

# 162

## SPIRITUAL MANIFESTATIONS

*"Now to each one the manifestation of the Spirit
is given for the common good."*
*Paul (I Corinthians, 12:7)*

With the revivification of pure Christianity, in the spiritist groups with Jesus, the same preoccupation exists, which use to torture the apprentices of the apostolic times, with regards to mediumship.

The majority of the workers involved in evangelization become anxious for the immediate development of their incipient faculties.

In certain centers they insist on an achievement superior to the possibility that they dispose of; in others, they dream of great phenomena.

The problem, however, does not lay in the exterior acquisitions.

Let each individual enrich his own intimate illumination, intensifying his spiritual powers, through knowledge and through love, and he will enter into the possession of eternal treasures in a natural way.

Many apprentices would like to be great clairvoyants or admirable prognosticators of the future, motivated by the prospect of superiority; however, they do not even deign to meditate on the sweat of this sublime achievement.

They are inclined toward profit but do not reflect over the effort to achieve it. In that regard, it is interesting to recall that Simon Peter, whose spirit felt so happy to be with the Glorious Master in the Tabor, was not able to withstand the anguish felt by his Friend flagellated in the Calvary.

It is justifiable for the disciple to hope and seek spiritual aggrandizement; however, whoever does have a humble spiritual faculty should not be unappreciative because a fellow student has a more expressive quality. Let each person work with the material they were given, convinced that the Supreme Lord does not take part in the activities of spiritual manifestations according to the human whims, but rather, according to its general utility and usefulness.

# 163

## BE THANKFUL

*"And be thankful."*
Paul (Colossians, 3:15)

It is odd to perceive the great number of the apprentices that are always intent on receiving blessings while, rarely, do we find anyone disposed to render them.

The spiritual resources, however, in its common mobilization, should obey the same system applied to the providences of a material order.

In the chapter dealing with the blessings of the soul, it is not correct to receive and waste senselessly; but rather, to be prudent and correct, so that the possibilities are not absorbed by the disorder or by injustice.

For this reason, in his instructions to the Christians of Colossus, the Apostle recommends that we be thankful.

Among the earnest disciples, the old habit of manifesting acknowledgement in a bombastic and flattering way is not justified. In the community of workers loyal to Jesus, to be thankful means to apply profitably the blessings received, not only for our fellow man, but for oneself as well.

For loving parents, the greatest appreciation from their children consists in an elevated understanding of the work, and of the life that they attest to.

Manifesting their gratitude to the Christ, the Apostles remained faithful until the last sacrifice; Paul of Tarsus received the call from the Master, and in a sign of happiness and of love, serves the Divine Cause by way of nameless sufferings for over thirty successive years.

To be grateful shall not be merely an expression of brilliant words; rather, it is to feel the grandeur of the action, the light of the benefits, the generosity of the confidence, and to correspond spontaneously, in extending to others the treasures of life.

# 164

## THE DEVIL

*"Have I not chosen you, the Twelve? Yet, one of you
is a devil." (John, 6:70)*

When Theology refers to the devil, the believer immediately imagines a being of absolute evil, dominating in an endless hell.

In the concept of the apprentice, the evil region is located in a distant sphere, in the entrails of tormented darkness.

Yes, the purgatorial zones are numerous and somber, terrible and painful, and according to the affirmation of Jesus Himself, the devil formed part of the apostolic services, remained near the disciples and one of them, would be constituted into a representation of the infernal spirit of evil himself. This said we must be aware that the term devil did not indicate, in the concept of the Master, a perverse giant, powerful and eternal in space and time. He designates man as if they were chained to the clumsiness of the inferior sentiment.

From that we can conclude that each human being presents certain percentage of diabolical expression, in the inferior part of his personality.

Satan symbolizes, then, the force that is contrary to righteousness.

When the individual discovers it, in his inner vast world, he understands the evil, combats it, avoids his intimate hell and develops the divine qualities that elevate him to a superior spirituality.

Great multitudes are submerged in secular desperation for not having been able to identify this truth.

And commenting on the passage of the Apostle John, we are obliged to ponder: "If among the twelve Apostles, there was one that would convert into a devil, in spite of the divine mission of the circle that was destined to the transformation of the world, how many already exist in each group of ordinary men on Earth?"

# 165

## FALSE SPEECHES

*"Do not merely listen to the word, and so deceive
yourselves. Do what it says." (James, 1:22)*

It is never too much to comment on the importance and the
sacred character of the word.

The Gospel itself affirms that in the beginning it was the
Verb, and if we examine closely the actual state of the world
today, we would recognize that all of the existing difficult
situations originate in the poor application of the power of the
verb.

False speeches fooled individuals, families and nations.
Some believed in vain promises, others in false theories, others
were still anticipating liberty without assuming the obligations.
Races, groups and people upon identifying the illusion, mutually
accuse one another, seeking the paternity of the faults.

The creation of the human verb has cost much blood and many tears. It would be impossible, at this time, to compute that painful price or determine the amount of time that will be required for the precious rescue.

In the whirlwind of the struggles, the friend of the Christ can seek refuge and take advantage of the treasure of the Gospel, benefiting his individual sphere.

Being able to comply with the words of the Master within us is the divine program. Without instituting that plan for salvation, the other services that are our responsibility would constitute sublimated theology, brilliant reasoning, magnificent literature, great admiration and respect from the inferior camp of the world, but never the required realization.

That is the reason why it is always dangerous to stop on the path, and listen to he who flees from the reality of our obligations.

# 166

# THE CURE OF HATRED

*"If your enemy is hungry, feed him; if he is thirsty, give
him something to drink. In doing this you will
heap burning coals on his head."*
Paul (Romans, 12:20)

The individual, generally speaking, when decided to be in the service of righteousness, will encounter rows of gratuitous adversaries wherever he or she goes, as invariably occurs to the light besieged by the antagonism of the shadows.

But sometimes, due to errors of the past or lack of the understanding of the present, they are confronted by more powerful enemies that become a constant menace to their tranquility. To have enemies of that kind is to endure a painful intimate illness, as the individual has not, as yet, become molded by living experiences in the Gospel.

As a rule, the good and faithful apprentice will develop his own strength to the maximum in favor of reconciliation; nevertheless, the greatest effort appears to be in vain. Impenetrability characterizes the heart of the other, and the best loving gestures pass by unperceived by him.

However, in order to counter that type of situation, the Divine Book offers a healthy recipe. It is not advisable to aggravate differences or further discussions and much less should the well-intentioned individual resort to flattery. Wait for the proper opportunity to manifest goodness.

From the minute that the offended individual forgets the dissention and returns toward love, the service for Jesus is restored; meanwhile, the perception of the offender is slow, and in most cases, he only understands the new light, when it is converted advantageously into his own personal circle.

A sincere disciple of the Christ easily frees himself from those inferior attachments; however, yesterday's antagonists can persist for a long time in the hardening of the heart. For this reason, by extending him all the goodness at the opportune moment, means to piling the renovating fire over his head, thereby, curing his hatred, which is filled with infernal expressions.

# 167

## UNDERSTANDING

*"Be transformed by the renewing of your mind."*
*Paul (Romans, 12:2)*

When we refer to the problem of spiritual transformation, the community of students of the Gospel agrees with us as to its necessity, but not all of them do seem to have perfect comprehension of the matter.

Invariably they all desire the modification; but the majority only aspires to a classified conventional change.

Those that have been less fortunate monetarily, seek to scale the control of material possibilities, the holders of the humble tasks fight over the higher positions, and in a disconcerting crescendo almost all intend the improper transformation of the opportunities which suit them, submerging into a disquieting disorder. The indispensable renovation is not that of an exterior nature. The devoted

Christian will be transformed not by external mannerism, and yes by the understanding, endowing his own mind with renewed light in new concepts.

Just as any earthly position requires the sincere application by any dedicated apprentice, the process of mental improvement requires constant effort in rightness and in knowledge.

Even here, it is important to recognize that discipline will be a decisive factor.

Do not become hardened, therefore, by the false notions that have already jeopardized you in the past.

Try to consider the structure of your reasoning today, before the circumstances that surround you. Question yourself as to what you gained in the Gospel, in order to analyze correctly, this or that occurrence in your path. Do this and the Lord's blessings will assist you in the illuminating reply to yourself.

# 168

## AT DAWN

*"Early on this first day of the week, while it was still dark,
Mary Magdalene went to the tomb and saw
that the stone had been removed from
the entrance." (John, 20:1)*

We should not forget the circumstances in which Mary of Magdalene receives the first message regarding the resurrection of the Master.

In the midst of the disorders and disenchantments of the small community, the great converted one wastes no time in sterile laments nor does she seek sleep to forget.

The companions had broken the pattern of confidence. Between the remorse of their own defection and the bitterness over the sacrificing of the Savior, whose sublime lesson, as yet, they were not able to learn, they became confused over negative attitudes. Contradictory thoughts and anguish pierced their hearts.

Magdalene, however, breaks the painful emotional veil that engulfs her steps. It is crucial not to yield under this burden transforming them, above all, in a basic element toward spiritual growth, and Mary resolved not to become fearful in the face of the pain. Because the Christ had been sacrificed on the cross, it would not be fair to condemn this loving memory to forgetfulness or to indifference.

Vigilant, attentive to her needs, prior to satisfying old conventions, she goes forth to confront the great obstacle, which was the grave. Very early, prior to awakening her very own friends, she encounters the radiant reply of the Eternal Life.

Recalling that symbolic occurrence, let us remember our prior falls, for having forgotten the "first day of the week," changing on every occasion "the earliest" for "the latest."

# 169

## EYES

*"With eyes full of adultery."*
*(II Peter, 2:14)*

"Eyes that are full of adultery" result in a stubborn illness in our evolutionary struggles.

Rare individuals utilize their two eyes as blessed lanterns, and very few utilize them as living instruments for sanctifying tasks in the necessary vigil.

The majority of the people try to take advantage of them in face of any scenario, in identifying it with the worst thing they possess.

Common man usually focuses intently on a determined situation, in order to fix his sight on a more favorable angle regarding inferior interests. If they go across a field they do not observe the merits of the collective landscape of life, but rather, the possibility of personal and immediate gain that exists. If they notice an affectionate feminine companion on the path that is proceeding not too far away, as a rule, they have undignified premeditations. If they come across companions who are involved in inferior activities, they are not seen as possible bearers of elevated ideas, but as concurring with their own inappropriate ideas.

Let us listen to the alarming cry of Simon Peter, and put aside the habit of analyzing with evil.

Optimistic eyes shall be able to extract sublime teachings in the most diverse situations on the path that they follow.

Let no one ever claim the need for vigilance in order to justify manifestations of malice. A prudent Christian knows himself how to view all problems, however, he never visualizes evil where evil does not exist.

# 170

# THE TONGUE

*"The tongue also is a fire."*
*(James, 3:6)*

Man's indifference justifies the bitter reference made by James in his epistle to his comrades.

The initiation of all the disasters on the planet, as a rule, is the result of the misuse of the tongue.

It is placed among the members, as a helm of a powerful ship, as recalled by the grand Apostle of Jerusalem.

Within its potential, there exist sacred recourses for just as the helm of smaller proportions was installed to steer.

The tongue withholds the divine spark of the verb; however, man, generally is accustomed to misguiding it from its edificating function, situating it in a marsh of subordinate reflection. For this very reason, we see it directing almost all of the delirium of mankind's suffering, hardened in its paltry objectives, and lacking humility and love.

The language of war is born in the dissatisfied criminal interests. The great social tragedies originate, on many occasions, in the conversation of inferior sentiments.

Seldom has man's tongue consoled or edificated his brothers; on the other hand, we recognize that its disposition is always ready to excite, dispute, depress, slander, accuse and hurt ruthlessly.

The sincere disciple will find in these statements of James a brilliant thesis for all experiences. And when night falls, at the end of each day, it will be proper to ask oneself: "Have I utilized my tongue on this day as Jesus utilized His?"

# 171

# THE LAW OF USAGE

*"When they all had enough to eat, he said to his disciples:*
*Gather the pieces that are left over. Let nothing*
*be wasted." (John 6:12)*

Once the "Law of usage" is observed, misery will flee from the human path.

To counter waste and selfishness, the work of each one of us is imperative because, once the equilibrium is identified, the service of economic justice will be complete, as long as goodwill exists among us.

The excerpt from the Gospel that describes the task of feeding the multitudes, signals important words of the Lord with regards to the left over bread, transmitting a teaching of profound significance to the disciples.

Generally, the earnest apprentice in the first dazzling understanding of the revealing faith desires to undo himself in the meritorious activities, not based on true harmony.

There we have, without a doubt, a laudable impulse, yet, even in the distribution of the material possessions it is indispensable to avoid lack of control or excesses.

The Father does not eliminate winter, because some of His children complain about the cold, but rather, He equalizes the situation by giving them covers.

Charity calls for enthusiasm; however, it also insists in generous discernment, so that the heart is not inclined toward indifference.

In the great assembly of the needy of the mount, with certainty, there was no lack of lazy and reckless persons ready to render useless the remainder of the bread without just cause. However, Jesus, before the frivolous manifested themselves, clearly recommended: "Gather the pieces that are left over. Let nothing be wasted." This, as in everything, man should recognize that the usage is understandable in the Law, despising abuse that is the mortal poison in all the fountains of life

## 172

# WHAT DO YOU AWAKEN?

*"As a result, people were transporting the sick into the
streets and laid them on beds and mats so that
at least Peter's shadow might fall on some
of them as he passed by." (Acts, 5:15)*

The conqueror of bloody glories spreads terror and wreckage wherever he goes.

The astute politician sows seeds of distrust and doubts.

The unfair judge awakens destructive fears.

The rebel spreads clouds of subtle poison.

The blasphemer injects evil dispositions in the listeners, provoking pernicious chatter.

The slanderer extends threads of darkness on their paths.

The lazy person dulls the energies of those he encounters, injecting deadening energies in them.

The liar causes disturbances and insecurity along his own steps.

The joker inspires and encourages hilarious tales, simply by his presence.

All of us through our thoughts, words, and actions, create a distinct atmosphere that identifies us in the eyes of others.

The shadow of Simon Peter, who had accepted the Christ and consecrated himself to Him, was sought after by the sufferers and the sick that found in it a special hope and relief, comfort and happiness.

Examine the topics and the attitudes that your presence awakens in people. With careful observation you will discover the quality of your shadow, and if you are interested in acquiring the illuminative values with Jesus, it will be easy for you to find your deficiencies and to correct them.

# 173

## HOW TO TESTIFY

*"But you will receive power when the Holy Spirit comes on you; and you will be my witnesses in Jerusalem, and in all Judea and Samaria, and to the ends of the earth." (Acts, 1:8)*

Truly, Jesus is the Savior of the World; however, He will not be able to liberate the Earth from the command of evil without the aid of those who seek salvation.

The Divine Master, therefore, requires auxiliary assistants, qualified as directors and witnesses, everywhere.

The improvement of souls without the education is impracticable, and the education requires legions of cooperators.

However, in order to perform the role of representatives of the Lord, in the sublime task of elevation, the external title achieved in the religious school is not enough. It is indispensable to obtain blessings from on High via the practice of our own duties, no matter how painful or difficult they may be.

Up to the present, we know very well on Earth, the power of dominating, governing, rejecting and injuring, of easy access in the field of life.

But few individuals make the effort of being deserving of the Celestial Power of Jesus, of obedience, in teaching; of loving, constructing for goodness; of waiting, working, and assisting unselfishly.

Without acquiring these resources, which identify us with the Divine Worker, and without having the opportunity of reflecting this on our fellow man, in spirit and in truth, through our constant efforts of personal application of the Gospel, we can personify excellent preachers, brilliant literary men or notable sympathizers of the Christian Doctrine, but, not His witnesses.

# 174

## SPIRITISM IN THE FAITH

*"And these signs will accompany those who believe: In my name they will drive out demons; they will speak in new tongues." Jesus (Mark, 16:17)*

Manifestations of spiritual life exist in all the foundations of the Divine Revelation in the most varied circles of faith.

Spiritism, therefore, in itself, ceases to be the surprise innovation of the times, but rather, depicted in the root of all religious schools.

Moses established contact with the spiritual sphere in the Sinai.

Jesus is seen by the disciples in the Tabor surrounded by illustrious souls.

The apostolic school establishes a relation with the Spirit of the Master after His death, and consolidates the redeeming Christianity in the world.

The martyrs of the amphitheaters abandon their flagellated bodies as they contemplated sublime visions.

Mohammed initiated his religious task upon hearing an invisible messenger.

Francis of Assisi perceived emissaries from Heaven, who exhorted him to a renovation of the Church.

Martin Luther registered the presence of beings from another world.

Teresa of Avila received the visit of discarnate friends, and is led to inspect regions of purgatory through the mediumistic phenomenon of out of body experience.

Signals from the Kingdom of the Spirits will follow the believers, affirms the Christ. In all the institutions of faith there are those who enjoy, who take good advantage of, who calculate, who criticize, who oversee. Those are, still, definite candidates for illumination and renovation. Those that believe, however, and accept the determinations of service that flows from on High, will be followed by the revealing account about immortality, wherever they are. In the name of the Lord, by emitting sanctifying vibrations, they will expel the forces of darkness and of evil, and will be easily recognized among the frightened men, because they will always speak in the new language of sacrifice, of peace, of renunciation, and of love.

# 175

## TREATMENT OF OBSESSION

*"Crowds gathered also from the towns around Jerusalem,
bringing their sick and those tormented by evil spirits,
and all of them were healed." (Acts, 5:16)*

The Christian Church of the first centuries did not hinder the redeeming ideas of the Christ in silvery glitter of the external worship.

It was alive, full of pleadings and answers.

Similarly, the Evangelical Spiritism today opens its benevolent doors to whoever is suffering or seeks the path of salvation.

It is interesting to note that the tremendous task ahead for the spiritists of the hour in the rescue of complex and painful obsessions, was intimately known by the Apostles. They counseled the perturbed spirits renovating, through the examples and through the teachings, not only the discarnates in severe suffering, but also, the sick mediums who were affected by their spiritual interferences.

From the very start of the doctrinaire task, the soul of Christianity is cognizant that the invisible beings, confused and unbalanced, roam the world producing psychic wounds to whoever is the recipient of their action, and is not unaware of the demanding task of conversion and spiritual elevation that is required to be realized. However, the religious dogmas have impeded its efficient service, for many centuries.

Presently, the primitive scenes of the Glad Tidings resurge.

Ignorant and unfortunate spiritual entities receive new light, and a new course in the loving homes that Christian Spiritism institutes, overcoming prior concepts and important difficulties.

The treatment of obsession, therefore, is not an eccentric task in our centers of renovating faith. It simply constitutes the continuing effort of salvation to all the wayward souls, which commenced in the luminous hands of Jesus.

# 176

## IN THE REVELATION OF LIFE

*"With great power the apostles continued to testify of the resurrection to the Lord Jesus, and much grace was upon them all." (Acts, 4:33)*

The closest companions of the Divine Master did not establish the community services over stagnant immobile principles. They cultivated order, hierarchy, and discipline; moreover, they also assisted the spirit of the people, distributing the goodness of the spiritual revelation according to the receptive capacity of each one of the candidates of the new faith.

To deny, at present, the legitimacy of the spiritist effort, in the name of the Christian Faith, is an ignorant or frivolous testimony.

The disciples of the Lord understood the importance of the certainty of life after death in order to triumph in the moral life. They witnessed the radical transformation in themselves, after the resurrection of their Heavenly Friend, upon recognizing that love and justice direct the being far beyond the tomb. For this very reason they would attract new companions, transmitting to them their conviction that the Master continued to live and was active beyond the grave.

For this reason the apostolic ministry did not become solely divided in the discussion of the intellectual problems of the faith and in adoring praise. The followers of the Christ supplied "with great power continued to testify of the resurrection to the Lord Jesus," and because of the love with which they devoted themselves to the task of salvation, there was within them "much grace."

Evangelical Spiritism arrives in order to mobilize the divine services that it enfolds, not only the consoling belief, but also the indisputable knowledge of immortality.

The dogmatic doctrines will continue aligning inoperative points of faith, freezing the ideas in obscured declarations; however, Christian Spiritism comes to restore, through its redeeming activities, the teaching of the individual resurrection, consecrated by the Divine Master, who Himself, returned from the shadows of death, in order to exalt the continuity of life.

177

# LET US GUARD OUR MENTAL HEALTH

*"Set your mind on things above, not on earthly things."*
*Paul (Colossians, 3:2)*

Primitive Christianity was not unaware of the necessity of a sound healthy mind enlightened by superior aspirations, in the lives of those who embrace the renovating essence of the Gospel.

The work of present notable thinkers finds its roots much earlier.

Today, those who deal with mediumistic phenomena know that the death of the flesh does not impose celestial pleasures.

The individual finds himself beyond the tomb with the virtues and defects, ideas and vices, to which he dedicated himself while in the physical body.

The criminal becomes drawn to the circle of his own crimes, when they are not chained to the accomplices of the original fault committed.

The miser is tied to the superfluous wealth that he abusively hoarded.

The proud remains tied to the fleeting titles.

The alcoholic makes the rounds looking for the possibility of satisfying the thirst that controls his centers of force.

He who has been passionate over capricious organizations "of the self" wastes long days to disassociate himself from the veil of illusion, in which his personality is segregated.

The program precedes the service.

The project charts the realization.

Thought is a radiating energy. If we spread it on Earth we will naturally be attached to the ground. Let us elevate it toward the Heights, and we will win the sublime spirituality.

Our spirit will reside wherever we project our thoughts, living bases of goodness and evil. For this very reason Paul stated wisely "Set your mind on things above."

## 178

# THE BATTLE WITHIN

*"Since you are going through the same struggle you saw*
*I had, and now hear that I still have."*
Paul (Philippians, 1:30)

In his youth, Paul did bear arms against common circumstances in order to consolidate his position and assert himself in the future of the race. He fought to surpass the intelligence of the youth of his time, distancing himself from many colleagues and companions. He argued with Doctors of Law, and was victorious. He tried and succeeded in obtaining a most enviable material situation. He fought to prove himself in the highest court of Jerusalem and overcame elderly instructors of the chosen people. He resolved to pursue those who he felt were enemies of the established order and multiplied his adversaries everywhere. He wounded, tormented, and complicated the life of some of his respectable friends, sentenced innocent people to nameless worries, and fought against sinners and saints, the just and the unjust.

However, a moment surged in which the Lord beckoned his spirit to another type of battle: the battle within.

When that time arrived, Paul of Tarsus become quiet and listened…

The sword broke in his hands forever. He no longer has arms to harass, but only to be helpful and to serve.

He travels in a modified manner, inversely. Instead of humiliating others he bows his own neck.

He goes through suffering and perfects himself through silence with the same disposition for work that characterized him in his era of blindness.

He is stoned, incarcerated, beaten, often misunderstood; however, he proceeds steadfast to the encounter of the Divine Renovation.

If you still have not battled with your inner self, the day will come when you will be called upon to similar service. Pray and be vigilant; prepare yourself and adapt your heart to humility and patience. Remember my brother, that not even Paul, who was graced by the personal visit of Jesus, was able to escape.

# 179

# LET US ACHIEVE UNDERSTANDING BY SERVING

*"At one time we too were foolish."*
Paul (Titus, 3:3)

The hammer is a true collaborator at the commencement of sculpturing; however, it cannot beat on the rock indiscriminately.

The bitter remedy establishes the cure of a sick body; however, science is required for the specific dosage.

No more, no less.

In the sowing of truth it is equally indispensable that we do not make thoughtless moves.

On Earth we do not breath in a home of angels.

We are millions of human beings in a labyrinth of clamorous debts from the past, and craving for the desired equation.

He who teaches with sincerity, naturally learned his lessons while crossing through difficult obstacles.

It is clear that excessive tolerance will result in the absence of a just defense; however, it is undeniable that in order to educate others we require an immense amount of patience and understanding.

Paul, who was incisive and strict, was not unaware of this reality.

As he is writing to Titus, he recalls his own doubts of another era in order to justify the serenity that must characterize our action while in service of the Redeeming Gospel.

We shall never reach our objectives by torturing wounds, indicating scars, commenting on defects, or lashing out thorns to another's face.

Comprehension and respect should precede our task everywhere.

Let us be reminded of our own passage through the lower circles and extend our fraternal arms to our brothers who struggle in the shadows.

If you feel that you are interested in the service to the Christ, bear in mind that He did not act as a promoter of accusations, but rather, in the rostrum of sacrifice till the moment of the cross, as an attorney representing the entire world.

# 180

## BELIEVE AND FOLLOW

*"As you sent me into the world, I have sent them into the world." Jesus (John, 17:18)*

My friend, if you embraced the Christian Spiritist task, in the name of the sublime faith, thirsting for a superior life, bear in mind that the Master sent you, a renewed heart, to the vast field of the world, in order to serve Him.

You will not only teach the righteous path. Your actions will be in accordance with the elevated principles that you preach.

You will dictate noble directives to others; but you will proceed within them, as well.

You will proclaim the necessity for good humor, as well as proceed on the path spreading happiness and blessings, even when you are misunderstood by all.

You will not be content in distributing coins and immediate benefits. You will always donate something of your own to whomsoever is in need.

It will not be enough to be forgiving. You will understand the offender, assisting in his transformation.

You shall not be critical. You will encounter unexpected resources to be useful.

You will not be demanding. You will take advantage of time in order to materialize the good thoughts that direct you.

You will not argue uselessly. You will find the path of service to others anywhere.

You will not simply combat evil with words. You will obtain goodness, planting it in everyone.

You will not condemn. You will discover the light of love in order to have it shining within your heart, until the sacrifice.

Pray and be vigilant.

Love and wait.

Serve and renounce.

If you are not disposed to take advantage of the lesson of the Divine Master, molding your very own life to His teachings, your faith will have been in vain.

This book was printed
in the Graphical Department of
FEDERAÇÃO ESPÍRITA BRASILEIRA
in the city of Rio de Janeiro,
Brazil, April, 2005.

www.febnet.org.br